2019

NEW TESTAMENT

STUDY & ACTIVITY GUIDE

By Shannon Foster

A companion guide to use along with
Come, Follow Me —
For Individuals and Families: New Testament 2019

www.theredheadedhostess.com

TABLE OF CONTENTS

IDEAS & TIPS

Below are some ideas and tips to help you teach your family and study the New Testament with this companion study guide. Read through them and see if any would work for you.

When to study. The schedule in *Come, Follow Me—For Individuals and Families: New Testament 2019* has you starting each new study on a Monday and ending on the following Sunday. If you are having Family Home Evening on a Monday night, this will not give you time to study the chapters and determine what is best for your family to learn. One possibility is during your personal scripture study, to study the next week's chapters and then be prepared to teach and study with your family the following week.

What to write. In this book we have taken each chapter in the New Testament and created "scripture boxes." At the top of each box is a title or summary of what is happening within those scripture verses. In the box you can record important doctrines and principles, events that are happening, impressions you received, or something that stood out to you. You could even draw pictures, make lists, or leave it blank! There is no right or wrong way. If you are stuck and having a hard time getting started, one question you could ask yourself is, "What would I want my children to learn from these verses?" That question can help you gain specific inspiration for your family not only now but in the future. For who knows what members of your posterity might read your notes in this book many years in the future?

Study helps. There will likely be times when you need additional resources to help you understand the wording and meaning of some verses. Church institute and seminary manuals can be excellent resources and are found online. There are many other good commentary books as well. Do your research to find trustworthy sources and then keep them close as you study, but YOU should be your first source. Before you turn to the other helps, strive to figure it out on your own. As you do this, your ability will improve and you will be open to receive inspiration specific to you and your family.

Write your own commentary. The scripture boxes in this book are designed to help you slow down and essentially write your own commentary. You have the capacity and ability to receive great insights. In fact, Edler Dallin H. Oaks said this: "*Last year a church member sent me a suggestion that someone prepare a book containing all General Authority interpretations of all verses in the scriptures. I replied that I thought this was not a good idea.... What we are seeking to accomplish... is not to magnify the standing of the prophets but to elevate the spirituality of our rank and file members. Like Moses, we declare, 'would God that all the Lord's people were prophets, and that the Lord would put his spirit upon them!' (Numbers 11:29). We encourage everyone to study the scriptures prayerfully and seek personal revelation to know the meaning for themselves.*" (Elder Dallin H. Oaks, "Scripture Reading and Revelation", BYU Studies Academy Meeting, January 29, 1993)

Teaching your family. You will determine what is the best time and way to teach your family these important chapters. One idea to consider (or adapt to fit your needs) is to have a full lesson on Monday night for Family Home Evening, and then mini lessons throughout the week for daily family scripture study. Your children could even be assigned a certain day of the week when they are in charge of the mini lesson and either choose to further teach something from the lesson on Monday, or find another scripture within the week's assigned chapters to teach.

Your home is a unique classroom. Your home has opportunities formal classrooms do not. For example, you do not have the time constraints a classroom has and you know your children better than a teacher could. Take advantage of these circumstances and consider the following ideas:

- Can you do something special with dinner or dessert? For example, during the Last Supper lesson you might serve some foods that Christ might have eaten that night, or during a lesson where you teach about Family History, you might serve some old family recipes.
- Can you do something, or go somewhere during the week that will further learning? - Is there a challenge you could give for the week and invite everyone to report during family dinner or family prayer?
- Could you challenge your older children to pick a scripture each week from the lesson and memorize it?

Invest in supplies. Children are visual learners, love to create, and will learn by doing. Throughout this guide we have given you several ideas of things they can make and do. Some items you might want to buy in bulk are: poster board, markers, and crayons. You will also want each of your children to have their own personal journals. You can use a simple notebook, or we have children journals available at www.theredheadedhostess.com. Our journals have illustrated tips for each lesson, but leave the majority of the page blank so you can use it as you wish. Most of our activity ideas in this book include journal activities for your children.

** We would love to see some of your study pages or pictures of your family learning these lessons. Please tag us on Instagram @redheadedhostess, or contact us through our website.*

WE ARE RESPONSIBLE FOR OUR OWN LEARNING

DECEMBER 31 - JANUARY 6

Study the first paragraph in *Come, Follow Me—For Individuals and Families: New Testament 2019* in this week's lesson. In the box below, record the teachings that stand out to you as well as any impressions you may receive. Be sure to make notes of any doctrines or principles you would like to discuss as a family in Family Home Evening, family scripture study or in another setting.

WHAT SEEK YE?

In your *Come, Follow Me—For Individuals and Families: New Testament 2019,* each week there are some ideas for personal scripture study. This book includes those ideas with space for you to keep your notes and impressions. Your *Come, Follow Me—For Individuals and Families: New Testament 2019* has more information about each topic, so you will want to always have these books side by side. This week there are four ideas. Keep your notes under each topic, and make sure to note when you want to discuss with your family.

1. *To truly learn from the Savior, I must accept His invitation, "Come, follow me."*

2. *I am responsible for my own learning.*

Elder David A. Bednar:

"As learners, you and I are to act and be doers of the word and not simply hearers who are only acted upon. Are you and I agents who act and seek learning by faith, or are we waiting to be taught and acted upon? … A learner exercising agency by acting in accordance with correct principles opens his or her heart to the Holy Ghost and invites His teaching, testifying power, and confirming witness. Learning by faith requires spiritual, mental, and physical exertion and not just passive reception" ("Seek Learning by Faith," Ensign, Sept. 2007, 64).

3 *I need to know the truth for myself.*

4 *What should I do when I have questions?*

Family Home Evening • Family Scripture Study

MAKE A PLAN

In the space below, make a plan on WHAT and HOW you would like to teach your family. As you plan, prayerfully consider each member of the family with their learning levels and personal needs. Also, consider how different family members can contribute to the teaching of the rest of the family. They could make visual aids, study a particular topic, and prepare to teach the family, research something, etc.

IDEAS FOR YOU:

- Teach about what a parable is (a simple story used to illustrate a moral or spiritual lesson).
- Lay out a poster board and draw 4 boxes on it. Have your children draw the four types of soil found in the Parable of the Sower (Matthew 13:3-9). Then by each box have them write what each type of soil represents (Matthew 13:18-23). Circle the box with the good soil and make a list of things you can do in your home to cultivate an environment in your home that would be labeled "good ground."
- Together, discuss the quote to the right.

"We counsel parents and children to give highest priority to family prayer, family home evening, gospel study and instruction, and wholesome family activities. However worthy and appropriate other demands or activities may be, they must not be permitted to displace the divinely-appointed duties that only parents and families can adequately perform." ("Letter from the First Presidency," Liahona, Dec. 1999, 1).

Family Council

The beginning of the new year is a good time to hold a family council about making your home more gospel-centered. Have your children make posters that display the teachings in Galatians 5:22–23 and Philippians 4:8. Have them teach about those scriptures and then discuss what your family can do this year to apply the teachings and have a gospel-centered home. Make a list of what you discuss below and consider making a family mission statement for 2019.

MATTHEW 1; LUKE 1

"Be it unto Me according to Thy Word"

JANUARY 7-13

As you study each set of verses, use the boxes to record what you are learning. Record the spiritual impressions you receive, the doctrinal truths you find, questions that come to mind, specific things you would like to teach your family, favorite phrases, etc. You can write, draw pictures, make diagrams... There is no right or wrong way.

The lineage of Christ **MATTHEW 1:1-17**	*Mary and Joseph* **MATTHEW 1:18-19**	*Joseph and an angel* **MATTHEW 1:20-23**
Marriage & birth **MATTHEW 1:24-25**	*The preface* **LUKE 1:1-4**	*Elisabeth and Zacharias* **LUKE 1:5-10**
Gabriel appears to Zacharias **LUKE 1:11-17**	*Gabriel appears to Zacharias* **LUKE 1:18-23**	*Elisabeth is pregnant* **LUKE 1:24-25**

Gabriel appears to Mary **LUKE 1:26-30**	*Gabriel appears to Mary* **LUKE 1:31-35**	*Gabriel appears to Mary* **LUKE 1:36-38**
Mary and Elisabeth **LUKE 1:39-45**	*Mary's praise* **LUKE 1:46-55**	*Birth of John the Baptist* **LUKE 1:56-63**
Birth of John the Baptist **LUKE 1:64-66**	*Zacharias' praise* **LUKE 1:67-79**	*John grows* **LUKE 1:80**

Study these sections in *Come, Follow Me—For Individuals and Families: New Testament 2019.* As you study, record the teachings that stand out to you as well as any impressions you may receive. Be sure to make notes of any doctrines or principles you would like to discuss as a family in family home evening, family scripture study or in another setting.

1 *Who were Matthew and Luke?*

The Gospels of Matthew and Luke

2 *Why did the Savior need to be born of a mortal mother and an immortal Father?*

Matthew 1:18–25; Luke 1:28–35

President Russell M. Nelson:

"[The Atonement of Jesus Christ] required a personal sacrifice by an immortal being not subject to death. Yet He must die and take up His own body again. The Savior was the only one who could accomplish this. From His mother He inherited power to die. From His Father He obtained power over death." ("Constancy amid Change," Ensign, Nov. 1993, 34).

3 *God's blessings come in His own time.*

Luke 1:5-25, 57-80

4 *The faithful willingly submit to God's will.*

Matthew 1:18–25; Luke 1:26–38

5 *Mary testifies of Jesus Christ's mission.*

Luke 1:46–55

FAMILY HOME EVENING • FAMILY SCRIPTURE STUDY

MAKE A PLAN

In the space below, make a plan on WHAT and HOW you would like to teach your family. As you plan, prayerfully consider each member of the family with their learning levels and personal needs. Also, consider how different family members can contribute to the teaching of the rest of the family. They could make visual aids, study a particular topic and prepare to teach the family, research something, etc.

TEACHING IDEAS FOR YOU:

- Cut up 42 pieces of paper (or get 42 3x5 cards) and write all of the names found in the lineage of Jesus Christ (starting with Abraham and ending with Jesus) as found in Matthew 1:1-17. Mix them up and have the children arrange them in the proper order.
- Have the children do their best to make a diagram of their own family history in their journals. Help them complete it if they need help. Tell stories of some of their ancestors and display inherited items you have, or have a family recipe that has been passed down (perhaps you could have a family dinner full of recipes from grandparents, great-grandparents, etc.).
- Have everyone write down some fears they have in their own journals. Read Matthew 1:20, Luke 1:13, and Luke 1:30 and then discuss why each of the people in the verses were fearful. Discuss why God would tell those people to "fear not" and have the children write down those reasons in their journals. Discuss why we should also "fear not." Have everyone write "FEAR NOT" over their list of fears in their journals.
- Read Luke 1:37 with your family. Share about a time when you had an experience in your own life when God blessed you so that something that seemed impossible was not. If you know any similar stories from your ancestors, share those as well. Watch the Bible Video on BibleVideos.org titled, "An Angel Foretells Christ's Birth to Mary".
- Pick a scripture from this lesson to memorize as a family. Talk about why you chose that scripture and why knowing that scripture by heart can help and bless your lives. Invite everyone to write the scripture in their own journals.

LUKE 2; MATTHEW 2

We Have Come to Worship Him

JANUARY 14-20

As you study each set of verses, use the boxes to record what you are learning. Record the spiritual impressions you receive, the doctrinal truths you find, questions that come to mind, specific things you would like to teach your family, favorite phrases, etc. You can write, draw pictures, make diagrams... There is no right or wrong way.

Bethlehem **LUKE 2:1-5**	*Birth of Christ* **LUKE 2:6-7**	*Angel to shepherds* **LUKE 2:8-12**
Multitude of angels **LUKE 2:13-14**	*Shepherds witness & testify* **LUKE 2:15-20**	*Mary & Joseph keep Law of Moses* **LUKE 2:21-24**
Simeon **LUKE 2:25-35**	*Anna* **LUKE 2:36-38**	*Christ grows* **LUKE 2:39-40**

Young Christ teaches at temple **LUKE 2:41-46**	*Young Christ teaches at temple* **LUKE 2:47-51**	*Christ grows* **LUKE 2:52**
Wise men come to Jerusalem **MATTHEW 2:1-2**	*Herod sends wise men to Bethlehem* **MATTHEW 2:3-8**	*Wise men find Christ child* **MATTHEW 2:9-12**
Flee to Egypt **MATTHEW 2:13-15**	*Herod orders babies to be killed* **MATTHEW 2:16-18**	*Family returns to Nazareth* **MATTHEW 2:19-23**

Study these sections in *Come, Follow Me—For Individuals and Families: New Testament 2019.* As you study, record the teachings that stand out to you as well as any impressions you may receive. Be sure to make notes of any doctrines or principles you would like to discuss as a family in family home evening, family scripture study or in another setting.

1 *Jesus Christ was born in humble circumstances.*

Luke 2:1–7

2 *There are many witnesses of the birth of Christ.*

Luke 2:8–38; Matthew 2:1–12

3 *Parents can receive revelation to protect their families.*

Matthew 2:13–23

4 *Even as a youth, Jesus was focused on doing His Father's will.*

Luke 2:40–52

5 *What is the Joseph Smith Translation?*

Joseph Smith Translation ("JST")

FAMILY HOME EVENING • FAMILY SCRIPTURE STUDY

MAKE A PLAN

In the space below, make a plan on WHAT and HOW you would like to teach your family. As you plan, prayerfully consider each member of the family with their learning levels and personal needs. Also, consider how different family members can contribute to the teaching of the rest of the family. They could make visual aids, study a particular topic and prepare to teach the family, research something, etc.

TEACHING IDEAS FOR YOU:

- Set out your family nativity and have each person select one of the nativity figures. Ask everyone to read about, and consider, what the experience of the birth of Christ might have been like for that person and how it could have increased their faith in Christ.
- Read through the words of the Primary songs "Mary's Lullaby" and/or "The Nativity Song." Have everyone listen for their favorite phrase and then share what that phrase is with everyone else. Sing the songs together. Have the children draw a picture of the phrase they chose in their own journals.
- Read about Jesus Christ at the temple in Luke 2: 46-49 or watch the Bible Video on BibleVideos.org titled, "Young Jesus Teaches in the Temple." Discuss what it means that Jesus was about His "Father's business." Have the children circle the capital "F" in Father and teach them that this means he was talking about Diety or Heavenly Father. Discuss what "business" Heavenly Father is concerned with and then look up Moses 1:39. Have your children write the whole scripture in their own journals and then talk about what "immortality" and "eternal life" are and help everyone memorize this verse. Make a poster that says "Helping Heavenly Father with His Work" at the top and make a list of things everyone can do that week to be like Christ by being about Heavenly Father's business. Set it somewhere visible and invite everyone to put their initials next to items on the list whenever they do that thing during the week. Review the list each night during dinner or another time.
- Set out a poster board and make four columns on it. Explain that Jesus was not born a man, but a baby, and He had to develop and grow just like we are developing and growing. Look up Luke 2:52 and at the top of each of the four columns write (or draw pictures) of the four ways Jesus developed. Talk about them one at a time and then together make a list of ways your family can also develop and increase in each of those four ways. Invite your children to make a list in their own journals.

JOHN 1

We Have Found the Messiah

JANUARY 21-27

As you study each set of verses, use the boxes to record what you are learning. Record the spiritual impressions you receive, the doctrinal truths you find, questions that come to mind, specific things you would like to teach your family, favorite phrases, etc. You can write, draw pictures, make diagrams... There is no right or wrong way.

Christ in the Premortal Life **JOHN 1:1-5**	*John the Baptist came to witness* **JOHN 1:6-8**	*Christ is the Light* **JOHN 1:9-10**
Those who receive Christ **JOHN 1:11-12**	*The Christ was born in the flesh* **JOHN 1:13-14**	*John the Baptist testifies of Christ* **JOHN 1:15-18**
John responds to priests and Levites **JOHN 1:19-22**	*John responds to priests and Levites* **JOHN 1:23-28**	*John introduces others to Christ* **JOHN 1:29-34**

John the Beloved and Andrew follow Christ **JOHN 1:35-37**	*"Come and see"* **JOHN 1:38-39**	*Andrew tells Peter* **JOHN 1:40-41**
Peter meets Christ **JOHN 1:42**	*Christ finds Philip* **JOHN 1:43-44**	*Philip finds Nathanael* **JOHN 1:45-46**
Nathanael meets Christ **JOHN 1:47-48**	*Nathanael believes Jesus is the Christ* **JOHN 1:49**	*Things they will yet see* **JOHN 1:50-51**

Study these sections in *Come, Follow Me—For Individuals and Families: New Testament 2019.* As you study, record the teachings that stand out to you as well as any impressions you may receive. Be sure to make notes of any doctrines or principles you would like to discuss as a family in family home evening, family scripture study or in another setting.

1 *Who was John?*

The Gospel of John

2 *Jesus Christ was "in the beginning with God."*

John 1:1-5

3 *Disciples of Jesus Christ bear witness of Him.*

John 1:1–18

4 *What does it mean to "become the sons of God"?*

John 1:12

5 *Has anyone seen God?*

John 1:18

6 *Who is Elias, and who is "that prophet"?*

John 1:19–23

FAMILY HOME EVENING • FAMILY SCRIPTURE STUDY

MAKE A PLAN

In the space below, make a plan on WHAT and HOW you would like to teach your family. As you plan, prayerfully consider each member of the family with their learning levels and personal needs. Also, consider how different family members can contribute to the teaching of the rest of the family. They could make visual aids, study a particular topic and prepare to teach the family, research something, etc.

TEACHING IDEAS FOR YOU:

- On a poster board, have the children draw a picture of Jesus Christ and a picture of John the Baptist. Together, read John 1:4-10 and have them write (or draw) everything they learn about Jesus by His picture, and then write (or draw) everything they learn about John the Baptist by his picture. Turn off the lights and have a lit candle in the middle of the table. Talk about what light does for us and why one of Christ's titles is "Light of the World". Have everyone share how the Savior has been a Light in their life.
- Have the children make their own paper dolls and props to act out the story in John 1:35-46. They will need to make the following: Jesus, John the Beloved (this is John's record and he doesn't mention his own name, but he is one of the disciples in vs. 37), Andrew, Jesus' house, Simon Peter (later known as the Apostle Peter), a sign that says "Galilee", Philip, Nathanael. Use their props to tell the story and then have them identify every doctrine and principle they can find in the story (make a list together).
- Tell your children that you are going to read a story in John 1:45-51, but first you want them to make a list of all of the words they don't understand. Once they make the list, look up the definitions of each word and write them next to their words. Read the story together, pausing at each word they identify, and help them understand what it means. Once you are done, ask them to retell the story in their own words. Discuss what Nahanael did to help him gain a testimony of Jesus Christ for himself. Have everyone share what they have done to gain their own testimonies of Jesus Christ. Encourage them to write those things in their personal journals.

MATTHEW 3; MARK 1; LUKE 3

Prepare Ye the Way of the Lord

JANUARY 28 - FEBRUARY 3

As you study each set of verses, use the boxes to record what you are learning. Record the spiritual impressions you receive, the doctrinal truths you find, questions that come to mind, specific things you would like to teach your family, favorite phrases, etc. You can write, draw pictures, make diagrams... There is no right or wrong way.

John the Baptist prepares the way MATTHEW 3:1-6	*John warns and preaches* MATTHEW 3:7-10	*John announces the coming of Christ* MATTHEW 3:11-12
Baptism of Christ MATTHEW 3:13-17	*John the Baptist prepares the way* MARK 1:1-6	*John announces the coming of Christ* MARK 1:7-8
Baptism of Christ MARK 1:9-11	*Mount of Temptations* MARK 1:12-13	*Jesus teaches the gospel* MARK 1:14-15

Disciples follow Christ **MARK 1:16-20**	*Jesus casts out an unclean spirit* **MARK 1:21-28**	*Jesus preaches and heals* **MARK 1:29-39**
Jesus cleanses a leper **MARK 1:40-45**	*John the Baptist prepares the way* **LUKE 3:1-8**	*John the Baptist prepares the way* **LUKE 3:9-18**
Herod imprisons John **LUKE 3:19-20**	*Jesus' baptism* **LUKE 3:21-22**	*Lineage of Christ* **LUKE 3:23-38**

January 28 - February 3

Study these sections in *Come, Follow Me—For Individuals and Families: New Testament 2019.* As you study, record the teachings that stand out to you as well as any impressions you may receive. Be sure to make notes of any doctrines or principles you would like to discuss as a family in family home evening, family scripture study or in another setting.

1 *Who was Mark?*

The Gospel of Mark
Bible Dictionary, "Mark"

2 *Repentance is a mighty change of mind and heart.*

Matthew 3:1–12; Mark 1:1–8; Luke 3:2–18

3 *Who were the Pharisees and Sadducees?*

Matthew 3:7; Luke 3:7
Bible Dictionary, "Pharisees"; "Sadducees"

4 *Jesus Christ was baptized to "fulfill all righteousness."*

Matthew 3:13–17; Mark 1:9–11; Luke 3:15–16, 21–22

5 *Does the Bible teach that the members of the Godhead are three separate beings?*

Matthew 3:16–17; Mark 1:9–11; Luke 3:21–22

FAMILY HOME EVENING • FAMILY SCRIPTURE STUDY

MAKE A PLAN

In the space below, make a plan on WHAT and HOW you would like to teach your family. As you plan, prayerfully consider each member of the family with their learning levels and personal needs. Also, consider how different family members can contribute to the teaching of the rest of the family. They could make visual aids, study a particular topic and prepare to teach the family, research something, etc.

TEACHING IDEAS FOR YOU:

- Have your children each make a book about the baptism of Jesus Christ. Staple seven pieces of paper together and have them make a front cover, and then number the six pages after the cover, pages one through six. On the bottom of page one write, "Matthew 3:13-14." On the bottom of page two write, "Matthew 3:15." And on the bottom of page three write, "Matthew 3:16." Instruct your children to read the scriptures and draw pictures and write captions that depict what is happening in those scriptures. Then on the last three pages tell them to add to their book something important about the story. Some ideas could be about the Godhead, baptism, the gift of the Holy Ghost, or about John holding the Aaronic Priesthood.
- Read Matthew 3:17 and tell a story about a time when you knew that Heavenly Father was pleased with you. Invite everyone else to tell a story of a time that they knew Heavenly Father was pleased with them. On a poster board make five columns and in column one write "today," in column two write, "this week," in column three write "this year," in column four write "1-10 years," and in column five write "in 10+ years" (you may want to adapt some of the time frames to meet your individual family member's needs). Write everyone's names down the left side of the poster, and then go through each column and discuss (and write down) some things each person can do that would be pleasing unto God within each time frame. So you would start with one family member and discuss some things they could do "today," some things they could do "this week," and so on, and continue until each family member has had a turn. Invite everyone to take notes in their personal journals.

MATTHEW 4; LUKE 4–5

The Spirit of the Lord Is upon Me

FEBRUARY 4–10

As you study each set of verses, use the boxes to record what you are learning. Record the spiritual impressions you receive, the doctrinal truths you find, questions that come to mind, specific things you would like to teach your family, favorite phrases, etc. You can write, draw pictures, make diagrams... There is no right or wrong way.

Jesus fasts for 40 days & nights **MATTHEW 4:1-2** ** Note the JSTs in verses 1-11*	*Satan tempts Christ* **MATTHEW 4:3-4**	*Satan tempts Christ again* **MATTHEW 4:5-7**
Satan tempts Christ a third time **MATTHEW 4:8-11**	*Christ fulfills prophecy* **MATTHEW 4:12-16**	*Christ begins his ministry* **MATTHEW 4:17**
Disciples chosen and called **MATTHEW 4:18-22**	*Jesus preaches and heals in Galilee* **MATTHEW 4:23-25**	*Satan tempts Christ* **LUKE 4:1-13**

Christ begins ministry **LUKE 4:14-15**	*Christ rejected in Nazareth* **LUKE 4:16-32**	*Christ casts out unclean spirit* **LUKE 4:33-37**
Christ heals and preaches **LUKE 4:38-44**	*Disciples follow Christ* **LUKE 5:1-11**	*Christ cleanses leper* **LUKE 5:12-16**
Christ heals and forgives paralytic **LUKE 5:17-26**	*Jesus eats with sinners* **LUKE 5:27-32**	*New wine in new bottles* **LUKE 5:33-39**

February 4-10

Study these sections in *Come, Follow Me—For Individuals and Families: New Testament 2019.* As you study, record the teachings that stand out to you as well as any impressions you may receive. Be sure to make notes of any doctrines or principles you would like to discuss as a family in family home evening, family scripture study or in another setting.

1 *Communing with God prepares me to serve Him.*

Matthew 4:1–2
JST Matthew 4: 1-2, footnote "b"

2 *Jesus Christ set the example for me by resisting temptation.*

Matthew 4:1–11; Luke 4:1–13

3 *Jesus Christ is the prophesied Messiah.*

Luke 4:16–32

4 *As I trust in the Lord, He can help me reach my divine potential.*

Matthew 4:18–22; Luke 5:1–11

FAMILY HOME EVENING • FAMILY SCRIPTURE STUDY

MAKE A PLAN

In the space below, make a plan on WHAT and HOW you would like to teach your family. As you plan, prayerfully consider each member of the family with their learning levels and personal needs. Also, consider how different family members can contribute to the teaching of the rest of the family. They could make visual aids, study a particular topic and prepare to teach the family, research something, etc.

TEACHING IDEAS FOR YOU:

- What is a food or treat that would tempt your children? Print several pictures of that food or treat and hang it all over the room. Decide on a few other food items that would not tempt them (maybe they don't like pickles or mushrooms) and print those pictures as well. When everyone gathers for the lesson they will probably begin expressing the desire to have the treat that is hanging around the room and will mention this many times. Explain that you knew that this was something they would want and you knew it would tempt them. Show them the other non-tempting pictures and explain that you knew them well enough not to hang these pictures around the room because it would not be tempting to them.
- Explain that you are going to study about a time when Satan tried to tempt Christ with very specific temptations, just like you specifically tempted them. On a poster board draw this grid:

	What Satan tempted Christ to do	*Pizza!* *(or whatever food or treat you are using to tempt)*	*How Christ responded to the temptation*
Matthew 4:3-4			
Matthew 4:5-7			
Matthew 4:8-11			

In the center column write the food or treat you printed and put up all over the room. This center column represents the individualized temptation that Satan was trying to use on Christ. Satan did not just give Christ random temptations, but he had carefully chosen three temptations that were fine-tuned for Christ. Study those scriptures together and fill in the grid by drawing or writing what you find. This can also be done in individual journals.
- Share and discuss this quote by President David O. McKay: ***"Classify them, and you will find that under one of those three nearly every given temptation that makes you and me spotted . . . comes to us as (1) a temptation of the appetite; (2) a yielding to the pride and fashion and vanity of those alienated from the things of God; or (3) a gratifying of the passion, or a desire for the riches of the world, or power among men"*** (in Conference Report, Oct. 1911, 59).
- Teach about the Premortal Life and who Satan is, and why he wants to tempt us.

JOHN 2-4

Ye Must Be Born Again

FEBRUARY 11-17

As you study each set of verses, use the boxes to record what you are learning. Record the spiritual impressions you receive, the doctrinal truths you find, questions that come to mind, specific things you would like to teach your family, favorite phrases, etc. You can write, draw pictures, make diagrams... There is no right or wrong way.

Jesus turns water into wine **JOHN 2:1-12**	*Jesus cleanses temple* **JOHN 2:13-17**	*Jesus teaches of His resurrection* **JOHN 2:18-22**
Many believe **JOHN 2:23-25**	*Nicodemus* **JOHN 3:1-6**	*Nicodemus* **JOHN 3:7-12**
Moses raised serpent as symbol of Christ **JOHN 3:13-15**	*God so loved the world...* **JOHN 3:16-22**	*John the Baptist teaches of Christ* **JOHN 3:23-36**

Baptisms **JOHN 4:1-2**	*Woman at the well* **JOHN 4:3-9**	*Woman at the well* **JOHN 4:10-15**
Woman at the well **JOHN 4:16-19**	*Woman at the well* **JOHN 4:20-26**	*Woman at the well* **JOHN 4:27-30**
Fields are ready to harvest **JOHN 4:31-38**	*Many Samaritans believe* **JOHN 4:39-42**	*Jesus heals nobelman's son* **JOHN 4:43-54**

John 2–4

FEBRUARY 11–17

Study these sections in *Come, Follow Me—For Individuals and Families: New Testament 2019.* As you study, record the teachings that stand out to you as well as any impressions you may receive. Be sure to make notes of any doctrines or principles you would like to discuss as a family in family home evening, family scripture study or in another setting.

1 *The power of Jesus Christ can change me.*

John 2:1–11

2 *I must be born again to enter the kingdom of God.*

John 3:1–21

3 *Heavenly Father shows His love for me through Jesus Christ.*

John 3:16–17

4 *Is God a spirit?*

John 4:24
JST John 4: 24, footnote "a"

5 *Christ offers me His living water.*

John 4:7–26

FAMILY HOME EVENING • FAMILY SCRIPTURE STUDY

MAKE A PLAN

In the space below, make a plan on WHAT and HOW you would like to teach your family. As you plan, prayerfully consider each member of the family with their learning levels and personal needs. Also, consider how different family members can contribute to the teaching of the rest of the family. They could make visual aids, study a particular topic and prepare to teach the family, research something, etc.

TEACHING IDEAS FOR YOU:

- Read about Nicodemus (John 3) and the Woman at the Well (John 4), and watch the videos (on BibleVideos.org) that go with those stories. The videos are called:
    - Jesus Teaches of Being Born Again (2:55)
    - Jesus Teaches a Samaritan Woman (4:07)
- When you are teaching about the Woman at the Well set out a large bucket full of water (preferably in the yard) and have your children try to carry it a long distance. Go back inside and explain that Jesus was really good at using everyday items and tasks to teach of important spiritual truths. This woman would have needed to go to the well every single day in order to have fresh water and it would have been a hard and tiring task. Christ is likening this to someone who is tirelessly looking for spiritual truth, and he is telling her that if she comes unto Him and His gospel, she will never thirst again. Testify of how the gospel of Jesus Christ has been like a well of living water in your life and has kept you from thirsting spiritually.

MATTHEW 5; LUKE 6

Blessed Are Ye

FEBRUARY 18–24

As you study each set of verses, use the boxes to record what you are learning. Record the spiritual impressions you receive, the doctrinal truths you find, questions that come to mind, specific things you would like to teach your family, favorite phrases, etc. You can write, draw pictures, make diagrams... There is no right or wrong way.

The Beatitudes **MATTHEW 5:1-4**	*The Beatitudes* **MATTHEW 5:5-8**	*The Beatitudes* **MATTHEW 5:9-12**
We are salt and light **MATTHEW 5:13-16**	*Christ replaces law of Moses with new law* **MATTHEW 5:17-20**	*Old vs. new law: Anger* **MATTHEW 5:21-26**
Old vs. new law: Adultery **MATTHEW 5:27-30**	*Old vs. new law: Oaths* **MATTHEW 5:31-37**	*Old vs. new law: Retaliation* **MATTHEW 5:38-42**
Old vs. new law: Love **MATTHEW 5:43-47**	*Be perfect* **MATTHEW 5:48**	*Christ breaks oral tradition concerning the Sabbath* **LUKE 6: 1-5**

Christ heals withered hand on Sabbath **LUKE 6:6-11**	*The Twelve Apostles* **LUKE 6:12-16**	*Blessings for righteous* **LUKE 6:17-23**
Woes **LUKE 6:24-26**	*Higher law of love* **LUKE 6:27-28**	*No retaliation* **LUKE 6:29-30**
Love your enemies / Do good **LUKE 6:31-35**	*Righteous judgment* **LUKE 6:36-38**	*Parable of blind leading blind* **LUKE 6:39-40**
Mote in eye **LUKE 6:41-42**	*Good vs. corrupt fruit* **LUKE 6:43-45**	*Wise vs. foolish man* **LUKE 6:46-49**

FEBRUARY 18–24

Study these sections in *Come, Follow Me—For Individuals and Families: New Testament 2019*. As you study, record the teachings that stand out to you as well as any impressions you may receive. Be sure to make notes of any doctrines or principles you would like to discuss as a family in family home evening, family scripture study or in another setting.

1 *Lasting happiness comes from living the way Jesus Christ taught.*

Matthew 5:1–12; Luke 6:20–26

2 *Why did the Savior compare His disciples to salt?*

Matthew 5:13

3 *The law of Christ supersedes the law of Moses.*

Matthew 5:17–48; Luke 6:27–35

4 *Does Heavenly Father really expect me to be perfect?*

Matthew 5:48

President Russell M. Nelson:

"The term perfect was translated from the Greek teleios, which means 'complete.' … The infinitive form of the verb is teleiono, which means 'to reach a distant end, to be fully developed, to consummate, or to finish.' Please note that the word does not imply 'freedom from error'; it implies 'achieving a distant objective.' …

"… The Lord taught, 'Ye are not able to abide the presence of God now … ; wherefore, continue in patience until ye are perfected' [D&C 67:13].

"We need not be dismayed if our earnest efforts toward perfection now seem so arduous and endless. Perfection is pending. It can come in full only after the Resurrection and only through the Lord. It awaits all who love him and keep his commandments" ("Perfection Pending," Ensign, Nov. 1995, 86, 88).

FAMILY HOME EVENING • FAMILY SCRIPTURE STUDY

MAKE A PLAN

In the space below, make a plan on WHAT and HOW you would like to teach your family. As you plan, prayerfully consider each member of the family with their learning levels and personal needs. Also, consider how different family members can contribute to the teaching of the rest of the family. They could make visual aids, study a particular topic and prepare to teach the family, research something, etc.

TEACHING IDEAS FOR YOU:

- Go to BibleVideos.org and watch the four videos for the Sermon on the Mount, two of them are for Matthew 5.
- Create posters of some of the righteous teachings found in Matthew 5 and Luke 6 (this can be done in personal journals or on paper). For example, someone could illustrate Matthew 5:14, "Ye are the light of the world." If it is warm outside you could do chalk art on the driveway. You could also mold Play-Doh to illustrate some of the teachings.
- Have your family select one of the Beatitudes that would bless your home if everyone worked to improve it. Give everyone a piece of paper and have everyone write the Beatitude on it and decorate the paper. On the back of the paper have them write what they think will happen if everyone works on that Beatitude over the next week. Hang everyone's papers throughout the home as constant reminders. Every night, talk about that Beatitude (you may want to find quotes and scriptures to share throughout that week) to help remind and encourage everyone to live it. At the end of the week, gather all the posters and read what everyone wrote on the back and discuss what blessings your family experienced while everyone worked on this Beatitude.
- Look through the teachings in Matthew 5 and Luke 6 and see if any stand out to you as being particulary applicable to difficult situations members of your family have encountered. Talk about each situation together and then look to those scriptures and discuss the teachings in the verses and how they can help us be Christlike in difficult moments.

MATTHEW 6-7

He Taught Them as One Having Authority

FEBRUARY 25–MARCH 3

As you study each set of verses, use the boxes to record what you are learning. Record the spiritual impressions you receive, the doctrinal truths you find, questions that come to mind, specific things you would like to teach your family, favorite phrases, etc. You can write, draw pictures, make diagrams... There is no right or wrong way.

Giving alms **MATTHEW 6:1-4**	*How to pray* **MATTHEW 6:5-8**	*The Lord's Prayer* **MATTHEW 6:9-15**
Fasting **MATTHEW 6:16-18**	*Treasures in heaven* **MATTHEW 6:19-24**	*Forsake all for missionary work* **MATTHEW 6:25-27** *JST Matthew 6: 25-27*
Forsake all for missionary work **MATTHEW 6:28-30**	*Forsake all for missionary work* **MATTHEW 6:31-34**	*Righteous judgment* **MATTHEW 7:1-5**

Holy things **MATTHEW 7:6**	*Ask and ye shall receive* **MATTHEW 7:7-8**	*Heavenly Father wants to bless us* **MATTHEW 7:9-11**
The Law of the Prophets **MATTHEW 7:12**	*The strait and narrow* **MATTHEW 7:13-14**	*How to determine a false prophet* **MATTHEW 7:15-20**
"I never knew you" **MATTHEW 7:21-23**	*The wise and foolish man* **MATTHEW 7:24-27**	*Jesus taught with authority* **MATTHEW 7:28-29**

February 25–March 3

Study these sections in *Come, Follow Me—For Individuals and Families: New Testament 2019.* As you study, record the teachings that stand out to you as well as any impressions you may receive. Be sure to make notes of any doctrines or principles you would like to discuss as a family in family home evening, family scripture study or in another setting.

1 *I should set my heart upon heavenly things.*

Matthew 6–7

2 *I can draw closer to God through humble, sincere prayer.*

Matthew 6–7

3 *What does it mean to use "vain repetitions" in prayer?*

Matthew 6:7

4 *Why don't we recite the Lord's Prayer?*

Matthew 6:9–13

5 *I should judge righteously.*

Matthew 7:1–5

6 *I come to know Jesus Christ by doing His will.*

Matthew 7:21–23

FAMILY HOME EVENING • FAMILY SCRIPTURE STUDY

MAKE A PLAN

In the space below, make a plan on WHAT and HOW you would like to teach your family. As you plan, prayerfully consider each member of the family with their learning levels and personal needs. Also, consider how different family members can contribute to the teaching of the rest of the family. They could make visual aids, study a particular topic and prepare to teach the family, research something, etc.

TEACHING IDEAS FOR YOU:

- Set out a poster and markers. Decide on the teachings you want to focus on as a family (use pages 34 and 35 to determine the teachings) and write a list of verses down the left side of the poster. As a family, study each set of verses and write what they teach next to the verses on the poster (they can also do this in their individual journals). Give everyone 3x5 cards and tell them to write situations they may encounter in their lives that these scriptures can help them with. For example, one might say, "My friend told me he never prays because he doesn't think Heavenly Father listens to him," and that situation could be discussed with Matthew 7:9-11. Gather everyone's cards and discuss each one.
- Decide on a scripture in Matthew 6-7 that your family wants to memorize. Have everyone write it in their journals and have someone write the scripture on a piece of paper and hang it somewhere in your home where everyone will see it often. Work on memorizing it together and practice reciting it throughout the week. Discuss situations that this scripture might help them in and why having it memorized can bless them.

MATTHEW 8-9; MARK 2-5

Thy Faith Hath Made Thee Whole

MARCH 4–10

As you study each set of verses, use the boxes to record what you are learning. Record the spiritual impressions you receive, the doctrinal truths you find, questions that come to mind, specific things you would like to teach your family, favorite phrases, etc. You can write, draw pictures, make diagrams... There is no right or wrong way.

Jesus heals a leper **MATTHEW 8:1-4**	*Jesus heals the centurion's servant* **MATTHEW 8:5-13**	*Jesus heals Peter's mother-in-law* **MATTHEW 8:14-15**	*Following Christ requires sacrifice* **MATTHEW 8:16-22**
Christ calms stormy sea **MATTHEW 8:23-27**	*Devils in herd of swine* **MATTHEW 8:28-34**	*Man with palsy is healed* **MATTHEW 9:1-7**	*Calling of Matthew* **MATTHEW 9:8-9**
Jesus eats with sinners **MATTHEW 9:10-13**	*New wine in new bottles* **MATTHEW 9:14-17**	*Jairus and his daughter* **MATTHEW 9:18-19**	*Woman with issue of blood* **MATTHEW 9:20-22**
Jairus' daughter **MATTHEW 9:23-25**	*Blind men healed* **MATTHEW 9:26-30**	*Devil cast out of man* **MATTHEW 9:31-34**	*Many healings* **MATTHEW 9:35-38**
Jesus heals a paralytic **MARK 2:1-12**	*Jesus calls sinner to repentance* **MARK 2:13-17**	*New wine in new bottles* **MARK 2:18-22**	*Jesus is Lord of the Sabbath* **MARK 2:23-28**

Jesus heals withered hand **MARK 3:1-6**	*Multitudes follow Christ* **MARK 3:7-12**	*Twelve Apostles called* **MARK 3:13-21**	*Devils cannot cast out devils* **MARK 3:22-27**
Unpardonable sin **MARK 3:28-30**	*Who is the family of Christ* **MARK 3:31-35**	*Parable of the Sower* **MARK 4:1-8**	*Why Christ used parables* **MARK 4:9-12**
Meaning of Parable of the Sower **MARK 4:13-20**	*All things will be revealed* **MARK 4:21-25**	*Parable of the seed growing secretly* **MARK 4:26-29**	*Parable of the Mustard Seed* **MARK 4:30-32**
Why Christ used parables **MARK 4:33-34**	*Jesus stills the storm* **MARK 4:35-41**	*Legion of devils enter swine* **MARK 5:1-20**	*Jairus* **MARK 5:21-24**
Woman with issue of blood **MARK 5:25-26**	*Woman with issue of blood* **MARK 5:27-30**	*Woman with issue of blood* **MARK 5:31-34**	*Jairus' daughter* **MARK 5:35-43**

March 4-10

Study these sections in *Come, Follow Me—For Individuals and Families: New Testament 2019.* As you study, record the teachings that stand out to you as well as any impressions you may receive. Be sure to make notes of any doctrines or principles you would like to discuss as a family in family home evening, family scripture study or in another setting.

1. *The Savior can heal infirmities and sicknesses.*
   Matthew 8–9; Mark 2; 5

2. *I can seek God's help even if I feel undeserving.*
   Matthew 8:5–13; Mark 5:24–34

3. *Being a disciple of Jesus Christ means that I put Him first in my life.*
   Matthew 8:18–22; Mark 3:31–35

4. *Jesus Christ has power to bring peace in the midst of life's storms.*
   Matthew 8:23–27; Mark 4:35–41

5. *I can defend my beliefs by teaching true principles.*
   Matthew 9:1–13; Mark 2:15–17

6. *Because of repentance, I can be of good cheer.*
   Matthew 9:1–8

FAMILY HOME EVENING • FAMILY SCRIPTURE STUDY

MAKE A PLAN

In the space below, make a plan on WHAT and HOW you would like to teach your family. As you plan, prayerfully consider each member of the family with their learning levels and personal needs. Also, consider how different family members can contribute to the teaching of the rest of the family. They could make visual aids, study a particular topic and prepare to teach the family, research something, etc.

TEACHING IDEAS FOR YOU:

- Divide the miracles in these chapters up among different family members (if you have young children, assign them to a parent). Give them 20 minutes to prepare a presentation about their miracle to the rest of the family. They can draw pictures, use objects, etc. Give everyone a chance to teach their miracle to the family while everyone takes notes in their personal journals about what they learned.
- Go to BibleVideos.org and watch some of these miracles with your family and talk about them and what each person learned.
- Explain that miracles can happen to us as well. Share a miracle that you have experienced or a story from your family or Church history.
- Do you have a statue or picture of Jesus Christ in your home? Put it in the center of the table. Take a stack of sticky notes and write different scripture references from this chapter that teach a truth about Jesus Christ (you can use pages 38 and 39 in this book for an overview of the references you could use). Read each scripture with your family and then write (or draw) on the sticky note a characteristic, gift, attitude, or quality of Jesus Christ, and then stick it on or by the statue or picture (have everyone write these in their own journals as well). Once you have several sticky notes done, have everyone select a Christlike quality they would like to perfect in themselves. Have everyone write down their quality and make some goals for the week. Throughout the week (during dinner or family scripture study) have everyone report how their goal is going.

MATTHEW 10-12; MARK 2; LUKE 7;11

These Twelve Jesus Sent Forth

MARCH 11–17

As you study each set of verses, use the boxes to record what you are learning. Record the spiritual impressions you receive, the doctrinal truths you find, questions that come to mind, specific things you would like to teach your family, favorite phrases, etc. You can write, draw pictures, make diagrams... There is no right or wrong way.

*** NOTE: MARK 2 WAS STUDIED ON PAGES 38 & 39, PLEASE REVIEW , OR ADD TO, YOUR NOTES ON THOSE PAGES.**

The Twelve Apostles **MATTHEW 10:1-4**	*Instructions to the Twelve* **MATTHEW 10:5-15**	*They will face persecution and trials* **MATTHEW 10:16-25**	*Teach the gospel in plainness* **MATTHEW 10:26-31**
Blessings to those who make covenants **MATTHEW 10:32-33**	*Christ did not come to bring peace* **MATTHEW 10:34-37**	*Many receive Christ by receiving His servants* **MATTHEW 10:38-42**	*Jesus speaks of John the Baptist* **MATTHEW 11:1-15**
Warnings to those who reject Christ **MATTHEW 11:16-24**	*The Father and the Son reveal each other* **MATTHEW 11:25-27**	*Take Christ's yoke upon us* **MATTHEW 11:28-30**	*Christ is Lord of the Sabbath* **MATTHEW 12:1-15**
Gentiles will accept Christ **MATTHEW 12:16-21**	*Casting out devils* **MATTHEW 12:22-30**	*Forgiveness* **MATTHEW 12:31-32**	*Good vs. evil fruit* **MATTHEW 12:33-37**

Adultery and sign seeking **MATTHEW 12:38-42**	*Unclean spirits* **MATTHEW 12:43-45**	*Who belongs to Jesus' family?* **MATTHEW 12:46-50**	*Christ heals Centurion's servant* **LUKE 7:1-10**
Widow's son raised from the dead **LUKE 7:11-17**	*Christ testifies of John the Baptist's mission* **LUKE 7:18-35**	*Woman anoints Jesus' feet* **LUKE 7:36-50**	*Jesus teaches how to pray* **LUKE 11:1-8**
Why we should ask **LUKE 11:9-13**	*Casting out devils* **LUKE 11:14-26**	*Blessings from keeping the word of God* **LUKE 11:27-28**	*Sign seeking* **LUKE 11:29-32**
Seek spiritual light **LUKE 11:33-36**	*Inner uncleanliness* **LUKE 11:37-44**	*Do not reject living and dead prophets* **LUKE 11:45-51**	*Motives of scribes and Pharisees* **LUKE 11:52-54**

Study these sections in *Come, Follow Me—For Individuals and Families: New Testament 2019*. As you study, record the teachings that stand out to you as well as any impressions you may receive. Be sure to make notes of any doctrines or principles you would like to discuss as a family in family home evening, family scripture study or in another setting.

1 *The Lord gives His servants power to do His work.*

Matthew 10

2 *When I am in the Lord's service, He will inspire me with what to say.*

Matthew 10:17–20

3 *What did Jesus mean by "I came not to send peace, but a sword"?*

Matthew 10:34–39

4 *Jesus Christ will give me rest when I rely on Him and His Atonement.*

Matthew 11:28–30

5 *As I am forgiven of my sins, my love for the Savior deepens.*

Luke 7:36–50

FAMILY HOME EVENING • FAMILY SCRIPTURE STUDY

MAKE A PLAN

In the space below, make a plan on WHAT and HOW you would like to teach your family. As you plan, prayerfully consider each member of the family with their learning levels and personal needs. Also, consider how different family members can contribute to the teaching of the rest of the family. They could make visual aids, study a particular topic and prepare to teach the family, research something, etc.

TEACHING IDEAS FOR YOU:

- Get a poster and draw a line down the middle. On the left side draw 12 boxes and have your children draw pictures of the Twelve Apostles. Find pictures of today's First Presidency and Twelve Apostles and print them so they are small enough to all fit on the right side of the poster. Have your children glue them on the poster and write their names under their pictures. Look up "Apostle" in the *Bible Dictionary* and write things on the posters that describe *both* groups on the poster. Have everyone write the names of the living Apostles in their journals, along with 3 or 4 important truths from the Bible Dictionary.
- Have a backpack full of heavy items (like books, rocks, canned foods, etc.), and set it in the middle of the table. Have several pieces of paper available and invite everyone to write down at least 10 hard things they might have to face in their lifetime (sickness, heartache, death of a loved one, etc.). Have everyone say what their 10 things are and put them in the backpack. One at a time, let everyone take turns carrying the backpack alone and talk about how difficult it is. Have everyone open up to Matthew 11:29. One at a time, have everyone put the backpack on again and read the scripture aloud. As they are reading it, have the strongest member of the family come beside the person who is wearing the backpack and lift up the pack, relieving much of the weight and pressure. Show a picture of two oxen yoked together, and discuss that a yoke keeps the oxen in step with one another and lightens the load tremendously. Discuss how this is mortality, and difficult things will certainly happen. But, if we are "yoked" to the Savior those burdens will feel significantly lighter and easier to bear.

MATTHEW 13; LUKE 8; 13

Who Hath Ears to Hear, Let Him Hear

MARCH 18–24

As you study each set of verses, use the boxes to record what you are learning. Record the spiritual impressions you receive, the doctrinal truths you find, questions that come to mind, specific things you would like to teach your family, favorite phrases, etc. You can write, draw pictures, make diagrams... There is no right or wrong way.

Parable of the Sower **MATTHEW 13:1-8**	*Why Christ uses parables* **MATTHEW 13:9-17**	*Meaning of Parable of the Sower* **MATTHEW 13:18-23**	*Parable of the Wheat and the Tares* **MATTHEW 13:24-30**
Parable of the Mustard Seed **MATTHEW 13:31-32**	*Parable of the Leaven* **MATTHEW 13:33**	*Christ fulfills prophecy* **MATTHEW 13:34-35**	*Meaning of Wheat and Tares* **MATTHEW 13:36-43**
Parable: Treasure hid in a field **MATTHEW 13:44**	*Parable: Pearl of Great Price* **MATTHEW 13:45-46**	*Parable: Net in the Sea* **MATTHEW 13:47-50**	*"Have ye understood"* **MATTHEW 13:51-53**
Jesus rejected at Nazareth **MATTHEW 13:54-58**	*Jesus travels and ministers* **LUKE 8:1-3**	*Parable of the Sower* **LUKE 8:4-8**	*Why Christ uses parables* **LUKE 8:9-10**
Meaning of Parable of the Sower **LUKE 8:11-15**	*All things will be revealed* **LUKE 8:16-18**	*Who is Jesus' family?* **LUKE 8:19-21**	*Christ stills the storm* **LUKE 8:22-25**

Jesus casts out devils **LUKE 8:26-39**	*Jairus* **LUKE 8:40-42**	*Woman with the issue of blood* **LUKE 8:43-48**
Jairus' daughter **LUKE 8:49-56**	*Repent or perish* **LUKE 13:1-5**	*Parable: The Barren Fig Tree* **LUKE 13:6-9**
Christ heals woman on Sabbath **LUKE 13:10-17**	*Parable: The Mustard Seed* **LUKE 13:18-19**	*Parable: The Leaven* **LUKE 13:20-21**
Are there few or many saved? **LUKE 13:22-30**	*Jesus to be slain* **LUKE 13:31-33**	*"O Jerusalem"* **LUKE 13:34-35**

MARCH 18–24

Study these sections in *Come, Follow Me—For Individuals and Families: New Testament 2019.* As you study, record the teachings that stand out to you as well as any impressions you may receive. Be sure to make notes of any doctrines or principles you would like to discuss as a family in family home evening, family scripture study or in another setting.

1 *What is "the kingdom of heaven" that Christ referred to in Matthew 13?*

Matthew 13

2 *My heart must be prepared to receive the word of God.*

Matthew 13:3–23; Luke 8:4–15

3 *Jesus' parables help me understand the growth and destiny of His Church.*

Matthew 13:24–35, 44–52

4 *The righteous must grow among the wicked until the end of the world.*

Matthew 13:24–30, 36–43

5 *In what ways did "certain women" minister to the Savior?*

Luke 8:1–3

FAMILY HOME EVENING • FAMILY SCRIPTURE STUDY

MAKE A PLAN

In the space below, make a plan on WHAT and HOW you would like to teach your family. As you plan, prayerfully consider each member of the family with their learning levels and personal needs. Also, consider how different family members can contribute to the teaching of the rest of the family. They could make visual aids, study a particular topic and prepare to teach the family, research something, etc.

TEACHING IDEAS FOR YOU:

- Go BibleVideos.org and watch "The Parable of the Sower" together. Have everyone draw the four kinds of ground in their journals.

As a family, discuss what you can each do to make sure your hearts and home would be considered "good ground." Make a list of those things in your journals and commit to act upon them. Share about a time when your heart was prepared to receive some truth and it grew inside you a "hundred-fold."

- Have a parable painting night. Set out paints and learn about some of the parables together and encourage everyone to pick one of the parables to illustrate. You can find great information about these parables and how they relate to one another in various articles on the Church's website.
- Set out items that represent the parables you are going to discuss (yeast [leaven], a pearl, a mustard seed, dirt, fig, and a fishing net. If you don't have those items, find pictures online and print them. Let everyone select one of the items and study the parable and teach everyone about how their item relates to gospel truths.

MATTHEW 14–15; MARK 6–7; JOHN 5–6

Be Not Afraid

MARCH 25–31

As you study each set of verses, use the boxes to record what you are learning. Record the spiritual impressions you receive, the doctrinal truths you find, questions that come to mind, specific things you would like to teach your family, favorite phrases, etc. You can write, draw pictures, make diagrams... There is no right or wrong way.

Herod beheads John the Baptist **MATTHEW 14:1-12**	*Jesus feeds 5,000* **MATTHEW 14:13-21**	*Disciples in ship during storm* **MATTHEW 14:22-27**	*Peter walks on water* **MATTHEW 14:28-33**
Christ heals many **MATTHEW 14:34-36**	*Scribes and Pharisees argue* **MATTHEW 15:1-20**	*Jesus heals Gentile's daughter* **MATTHEW 15:21-28**	*Christ heals many* **MATTHEW 15:29-31**
Jesus feeds 4,000 **MATTHEW 15:32-39**	*Jesus rejected at Nazareth* **MARK 6:1-6**	*Jesus sends Apostles out to labor* **MARK 6:7-13**	*Herod fears John the Baptist has risen* **MARK 6:14-16**
Herod fears John **MARK 6:17-20**	*Herod beheads John the Baptist* **MARK 6:21-29**	*Jesus feeds 5,000* **MARK 6:30-46**	*Jesus walks on water* **MARK 6:47-52**
Jesus heals many **MARK 6:53-56**	*Pharisees false traditions* **MARK 7:1-23**	*Jesus heals Gentile's daughter* **MARK 7:24-30**	*Miraculous healings* **MARK 7:31-37**

Jesus heals man on Sabbath **JOHN 5:1-15**	*Honoring the Son is honoring the Father* **JOHN 5:16-24**	*Gospel will be taken to the dead* **JOHN 5:25**
Christ as Judge **JOHN 5:26-30**	*Law of witnesses* **JOHN 5:31-38**	*Scriptures bring us to Christ* **JOHN 5:39-47**
Jesus feeds 5,000 **JOHN 6:1-15**	*Jesus walks on the Sea of Galilee* **JOHN 6:16-21**	*Multitudes seek Jesus* **JOHN 6:22-27**
Jesus is the Bread of Life **JOHN 6:28-59**	*Some are offended and stop following Jesus* **JOHN 6:60-66**	*Others ask, "to whom shall we go?"* **JOHN 6:67-71**

March 25–31

Study these sections in *Come, Follow Me—For Individuals and Families: New Testament 2019*. As you study, record the teachings that stand out to you as well as any impressions you may receive. Be sure to make notes of any doctrines or principles you would like to discuss as a family in family home evening, family scripture study or in another setting.

1 *Jesus Christ honors His Father.*

John 5:17–47

2 *The Savior can magnify my humble offerings to accomplish His purposes.*

Matthew 14:16–21; Mark 6:33–44; John 6:5–14

3 *Jesus Christ invites me to set aside my fears and doubts and exercise faith in Him.*

Matthew 14:22–33; Mark 6:45–52; John 6:15–21

4 *As a disciple of Jesus Christ, I must be willing to believe and accept the truth, even when it is hard to do.*

John 6:22–71

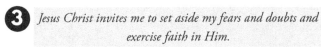

FAMILY HOME EVENING • FAMILY SCRIPTURE STUDY

MAKE A PLAN

In the space below, make a plan on WHAT and HOW you would like to teach your family. As you plan, prayerfully consider each member of the family with their learning levels and personal needs. Also, consider how different family members can contribute to the teaching of the rest of the family. They could make visual aids, study a particular topic and prepare to teach the family, research something, etc.

TEACHING IDEAS FOR YOU:

- Display the following items: Basket of bread and cutouts of fish, water, a blanket on the floor. Go to BibleVideos.org and watch the following three videos together, "The Feeding of the 5,000," "Wherefore Didst Thou Doubt?" (Peter walks on water), and "Jesus Heals the Lame Man on the Sabbath." Have everyone write or draw about each story in their personal journals. Discuss each story and pay special attention to the actions people took to follow Christ (for example: the 5,000 stayed [they didn't leave to find food on their own] so they were there for the miracle, Peter left the boat [even though he sank, he still walked on water], and the lame man stood up [he could have just lain there, not believing he could stand]). Discuss how these stories are full of people who exercised their faith in Christ and because they acted on their faith, they received evidences that Jesus was the Savior. Now show the Bible Video, "I am the Bread of Life" and discuss that Christ is the only one who can nourish us. Any other source we turn to will not be able to nourish us. Share some experiences you have had where you have acted upon your faith in Jesus Christ and received great blessings in return.
- Have a variety of bread, or even bread and fish for dinner. Teaching in the home provides unique experiences that your children could not experience in a classroom and will help this lesson stand out in their minds.

MATTHEW 16–17; MARK 9; LUKE 9

Thou Art the Christ

APRIL 1–14

As you study each set of verses, use the boxes to record what you are learning. Record the spiritual impressions you receive, the doctrinal truths you find, questions that come to mind, specific things you would like to teach your family, favorite phrases, etc. You can write, draw pictures, make diagrams... There is no right or wrong way.

Beware of the leaven of Pharisees & Sadducees **MATTHEW 16:1-12**	*"Thou art the Christ"* **MATTHEW 16:13-17**	*Church founded on rock of revelation* **MATTHEW 16:18-20**	*Christ rebukes Peter* **MATTHEW 16:21-23**
The worth of a soul **MATTHEW 16:24-26**	*Rewards to come* **MATTHEW 16:27-28**	*Mount of Transfiguration* **MATTHEW 17:1-13**	*Importance of fasting and prayer* **MATTHEW 17:14-21**
Jesus foretells death and resurrection **MATTHEW 17:22-23**	*Coin in fish's mouth* **MATTHEW 17:24-27**	*Mount of Transfiguration* **MARK 9:1-10**	*Elias* **MARK 9:11-13**
Jesus heals child **MARK 9:14-29**	*Jesus foretells death and resurrection* **MARK 9:30-32**	*Become as a little child* **MARK 9:33-37**	*The righteous work miracles* **MARK 9:38-40**

Receive Christ by receiving His servants **MARK 9:41**	*Consequences for those who offend children* **MARK 9:42-50**	*Jesus sends Twelve Apostles out to preach* **LUKE 9:1-6**	*Herod fears John the Baptist has risen from dead* **LUKE 9:7-9**
Jesus feeds the 5,000 **LUKE 9:10-17**	*"Whom say ye that I am?"* **LUKE 9:18-20**	*Jesus foretells His death and resurrection* **LUKE 9:21-22**	*The worth of a soul* **LUKE 9:23-25**
Those ashamed of Christ **LUKE 9:26**	*Mount of Transfiguration* **LUKE 9:27-36**	*Jesus casts out devils* **LUKE 9:37-43**	*Jesus foretells of His death* **LUKE 9:44-45**
Who is the greatest? **LUKE 9:46-48**	*Only righteous can cast out devils* **LUKE 9:49-50**	*Jesus came to save, not to destroy* **LUKE 9:51-56**	*True discipleship* **LUKE 9:57-62**

April 1–14

Study these sections in *Come, Follow Me—For Individuals and Families: New Testament 2019*. As you study, record the teachings that stand out to you as well as any impressions you may receive. Be sure to make notes of any doctrines or principles you would like to discuss as a family in family home evening, family scripture study or in another setting.

❶ *A testimony of Jesus Christ comes by revelation.*

Matthew 16:13–17; Luke 9:18–21

❷ *What happened on the Mount of Transfiguration?*

Matthew 17:1–9; Mark 9:2–10; Luke 9:28–36

❸ *What are the "keys of the kingdom of heaven"?*

Matthew 16:13–19; 17:1–9

❹ *When seeking greater faith, I must first hold on to the faith I already have.*

Matthew 17:14–21; Mark 9:14–29

FAMILY HOME EVENING • FAMILY SCRIPTURE STUDY

MAKE A PLAN

In the space below, make a plan on WHAT and HOW you would like to teach your family. As you plan, prayerfully consider each member of the family with their learning levels and personal needs. Also, consider how different family members can contribute to the teaching of the rest of the family. They could make visual aids, study a particular topic and prepare to teach the family, research something, etc.

TEACHING IDEAS FOR YOU:

- Set a picture of Christ up for all to see. Ask "Who is Christ?". Have everyone write their answers in their journals. Ask them how some people in the world might answer that question (he was a prophet, but not the Messiah, he is a legend that is not real, etc.). Share any experiences you might have had talking to someone who had a different belief in Christ than you have. Then ask, "Who do YOU say Christ is?". Watch the Bible Video on BibleVideos.org titled, "Thou Art the Christ." Roleplay some scenarios when others might approach your children with a different belief.
- There is an excellent YouTube video called, "House on Rock and Sand.wmv." Review that video, and if you have the supplies you can repeat that activity with your family. Otherwise, you can show them the YouTube video. After you watch the video, read Matthew 16:16-19. Explain that many people think that Christ is telling Peter he is going to lead the Church after Christ's death (which he does), but if you look at verse 18 when Christ says, "upon this rock I will build my church," the "this" he is referring to is in vs. 17 which is talking about the revelation Peter had received. So *revelation* is the rock the Church will be built upon. Look back to the object lesson with the houses on the rock and sand and ask why prophets receiving revelation is a foundation of rock (instead of voting on decisions for the church or methods like that). You can share this quote from Joseph Smith, "Jesus in His teachings says, 'Upon this rock I will build my Church. …' [Matthew 16:18.] What rock? Revelation" (Teachings of Presidents of the Church: Joseph Smith [2007], 195).

EASTER

O Grave, Where Is Thy Victory?

APRIL 15–21

One of the suggestions in *Come, Follow Me—For Individuals and Families: New Testament 2019* is to spend time each day reading about the last week of Christ's life. We have given you spaces to study and record what stands out to you. You could study one section each day this week.

TRIUMPHAL ENTRY INTO JERUSALEM

Matthew 21:6–11

CLEANSING THE TEMPLE

Matthew 21:12–16

TEACHING IN JERUSALEM

Matthew 21–23

CONTINUED TEACHING

Matthew 24–25

THE PASSOVER AND CHRIST'S SUFFERING IN THE GARDEN OF GETHSEMANE

Matthew 26

TRIAL, CRUCIFIXION, AND BURIAL

Matthew 27:1–61

CHRIST'S BODY LIES IN THE TOMB WHILE HIS SPIRIT MINISTERS IN THE SPIRIT WORLD

Matthew 27:62–66
D&C 138

THE APPEARANCE OF THE RESURRECTED CHRIST

Matthew 28:1–10

WITNESSES
OF THE RESURRECTION

What can you learn from those who were witnesses of Christ's resurrection? Write about each experience, what you think it might have been like for them, and how their experience can strengthen your faith and testimony in the resurrection of Jesus Christ.

Matthew 28:1–10	*Luke 24:13–35*
John 20:19–29	*1 Corinthians 15:1–8, 55*
3 Nephi 11	*Mormon 1:15*
Ether 12:38–39	*Doctrine and Covenants 76:19–24*
Doctrine and Covenants 110:1-10	*Joseph Smith—History 1:15–17*

FAMILY HOME EVENING • FAMILY SCRIPTURE STUDY

MAKE A PLAN

In the space below, make a plan on WHAT and HOW you would like to teach your family. As you plan, prayerfully consider each member of the family with their learning levels and personal needs. Also, consider how different family members can contribute to the teaching of the rest of the family. They could make visual aids, study a particular topic and prepare to teach the family, research something, etc.

TEACHING IDEAS FOR YOU:

- Watch the Bible Video (on BibleVideos.org) titled, "The Last Supper" and throughout the week watch that video and the next 13 videos until the video titled, "Blessed Are They That Have Not Seen, and Yet Have Believed." In their personal journals, invite your younger children to draw something they saw or learned after each video and use their drawings to review the story of the resurrection on Easter.
- Consider having a traditional Passover dinner together as a family. Teach about how the Passover helped the Jews remember what the Lord had done for them in Egypt and helped them look forward to the coming of the Messiah. Just before Christ's death, He introduced the Sacrament during the Last Supper to help us look back and remember His sacrifice. From that point on, would Christians no longer hold the Passover, but instead would participate in the Sacrament.
- Break up "The Living Christ: The Testimony of the Apostles" into small sections that your children can memorize. Hang up each section and have them sign their name next to each section they have memorized and recited to you.

MATTHEW 18; LUKE 10

What Shall I Do to Inherit Eternal Life?

APRIL 22–28

As you study each set of verses, use the boxes to record what you are learning. Record the spiritual impressions you receive, the doctrinal truths you find, questions that come to mind, specific things you would like to teach your family, favorite phrases, etc. You can write, draw pictures, make diagrams... There is no right or wrong way.

Become as little children **MATTHEW 18:1-6**	*Those who try to lead you astray* **MATTHEW 18:7-10**	*Parable of the Lost Sheep* **MATTHEW 18:11-14**
Forgive one another **MATTHEW 18:15-17**	*Priesthood keys* **MATTHEW 18:18**	*All things are possible* **MATTHEW 18:19-20**
Forgiveness **MATTHEW 18:21-22**	*The Parable of the Unmerciful Servant* **MATTHEW 18:23-27**	*The Parable of the Unmerciful Servant* **MATTHEW 18:28-35**

Seventy go forth to preach **LUKE 10:1-11**	*A warning* **LUKE 10:12-16**	*Power given to seventy* **LUKE 10:17-20**
The Father and Son reveal each other **LUKE 10:21-22**	*Why Jesus taught in parables* **LUKE 10:23-24**	*A lawyer asks Jesus how to inherit eternal life* **LUKE 10:25-29**
The Parable of the Good Samaritan **LUKE 10:30-35**	*The Parable of the Good Samaritan* **LUKE 10:36-37**	*Mary and Martha* **LUKE 10:38-42**

Study these sections in *Come, Follow Me—For Individuals and Families: New Testament 2019.* As you study, record the teachings that stand out to you as well as any impressions you may receive. Be sure to make notes of any doctrines or principles you would like to discuss as a family in family home evening, family scripture study or in another setting.

1 *I must forgive others if I am to receive forgiveness from the Lord.*

Matthew 18:21–35

2 *Who are the Seventy?*

Luke 10:1–20

3 *To obtain eternal life, I must love God and love my neighbor as myself.*

Luke 10:25–37

4 *We choose "that good part" by making choices that lead to eternal life.*

Luke 10:38–42

FAMILY HOME EVENING • FAMILY SCRIPTURE STUDY

MAKE A PLAN

In the space below, make a plan on WHAT and HOW you would like to teach your family. As you plan, prayerfully consider each member of the family with their learning levels and personal needs. Also, consider how different family members can contribute to the teaching of the rest of the family. They could make visual aids, study a particular topic and prepare to teach the family, research something, etc.

TEACHING IDEAS FOR YOU:

- Watch the Bible Video on BibleVideos.org titled, "Jesus Teaches that We Must Become as Little Children." If you have a little child in your home, have them stand by you (if you have more than one little child, do this activity with each of them, one at a time). Have some sticky notes nearby and ask everyone to tell you some Christlike traits that the child has. Write each trait on a sticky note and stick them on him or her. After each sticky note is in place, explain that little children naturally have many Christlike qualities and characteristics that we can all learn from, so Christ is telling us to try to become like them. Invite everyone to choose three traits they would like to work on perfecting in themselves, and write those traits in their journals. Encourage them to choose one trait to focus on during the week, and suggest that they record their progress in their journals.

- Ask your children the question that the lawyer asked Christ in Luke 10:25. Talk about what Eternal Life is and then read Christ's response to the question. Watch the Bible Video, "The Parable of the Good Samaritan," and then ask everyone to draw the story in their own journals. Explain that we might not come across someone that is wounded on the side of the road, but there are those all around us who are in pain or need. Together, make a list of people in your lives that you could help as a family or individually and make a plan on how you can help them.

JOHN 7–10

I Am the Good Shepherd

APRIL 29- MAY 5

As you study each set of verses, use the boxes to record what you are learning. Record the spiritual impressions you receive, the doctrinal truths you find, questions that come to mind, specific things you would like to teach your family, favorite phrases, etc. You can write, draw pictures, make diagrams... There is no right or wrong way.

Some Jews seek to kill Christ **JOHN 7:1**	*Jesus' kinsmen do not believe Him* **JOHN 7:2-9**	*Jews search for Christ* **JOHN 7:10-13**	*Jesus teaches at the temple* **JOHN 7:14-24**
Jesus teaches at the temple **JOHN 7:25-31**	*Jesus teaches at the temple* **JOHN 7:32-39**	*Diverse opinions about Christ* **JOHN 7:40-53**	*Woman taken in adultery* **JOHN 8:1-11**
Christ is the light of the world **JOHN 8:12**	*Christ speaks to the Pharisees* **JOHN 8:13-19**	*Christ speaks to the Pharisees* **JOHN 8:20-25**	*Christ speaks to the Pharisees* **JOHN 8:26-30**
Christ teaches those who believe Him **JOHN 8:31-45**	*Christ teaches those who believe Him* **JOHN 8:46-59**	*Jesus heals a blind man* **JOHN 9:1-7**	*Neighbors question blind man* **JOHN 9:8-12**

Blind man taken to Pharisees **JOHN 9:13-15**	*Objections to Christ healing on Sabbath* **JOHN 9:16**	*Blind man's parents* **JOHN 9:17-23**	*Blind man testifies* **JOHN 9:24-33**
Blind man cast out **JOHN 9:34**	*Jesus finds blind man* **JOHN 9:35-39**	*Jesus accuses Pharisees* **JOHN 9:40-41**	*Christ is the Good Shepherd* **JOHN 10:1-4**
Christ is the Good Shepherd **JOHN 10:5-10**	*Christ is the Good Shepherd* **JOHN 10:11-14**	*Christ is the Good Shepherd* **JOHN 10:15-18**	*Diverse opinions about Christ* **JOHN 10:19-21**
Christ teaches at the temple **JOHN 10:22-27**	*Christ teaches at the temple* **JOHN 10:28-32**	*Christ teaches at the temple* **JOHN 10:33-38**	*Christ teaches at the temple* **JOHN 10:39-42**

April 29–May 5

Study these sections in *Come, Follow Me—For Individuals and Families: New Testament 2019*. As you study, record the teachings that stand out to you as well as any impressions you may receive. Be sure to make notes of any doctrines or principles you would like to discuss as a family in family home evening, family scripture study or in another setting.

1 *As I live the truths taught by Jesus Christ, I will come to know they are true.*

John 7:14–17

2 *The Savior's mercy is available to all.*

John 8:2–11

3 *Why were the Jews offended when Jesus said, "Before Abraham was, I am"?*

John 8:58–59

4 *Through our challenges, God can manifest Himself in our lives.*

John 9

5 *Who are the "other sheep" the Savior referred to in John 10:16?*

John 10:16

FAMILY HOME EVENING • FAMILY SCRIPTURE STUDY

MAKE A PLAN

In the space below, make a plan on WHAT and HOW you would like to teach your family. As you plan, prayerfully consider each member of the family with their learning levels and personal needs. Also, consider how different family members can contribute to the teaching of the rest of the family. They could make visual aids, study a particular topic and prepare to teach the family, research something, etc.

TEACHING IDEAS FOR YOU:

- Take turns blindfolding different members of your family and give them simple tasks to do (put something away, sit in a specific chair, get a glass of water, etc.). Explain that you are going to learn about someone in the scriptures who was blind. On a poster board, or in personal journals, make a list of what you imagine life might have been like in that day for someone who was blind. You could start by going through a typical day (starting with waking up). Remember that they didn't have the conveniences that we have today, like running water, refrigeration, and electricity; so imagine what each day might have been like for them as they tried to meet their daily needs. Once you have made a pretty good list, read John 9 together, and then go to the Bible Videos on BibleVideos.org and watch the video for John 9 titled, "Jesus Heals a Man Born Blind." Pause the video after the man is healed and look at the list(s) you made and have a quick discussion about how this man's life is about to change. After you watch the remainder of the video, let everyone share the additional lessons they learned, as well as their favorite part of the video.
- As you teach about Christ being the Good Shepherd, you can create a fun visual with some of your children's toys. Use blocks to create a sheep pen or a sheepfold (make sure to leave a door). Or you can search "sheepfold" on the internet to show your children what it looked like and have them use Play-Doh to create a sheepfold. Use cotton balls for sheep and a shepherd from your nativity. You will also need a hired worker (a hireling), a thief, and a wolf (so either have your children make some or use some toy figures you might have). Use these as you read John 10:1-18, and John 10:27-29. At the end, replace the sheep with pictures of members of your family and then watch the Bible Video on BibleVideos.org titled, "The Good Shepherd and Other Sheep I Have," and then talk about how these scriptures apply to you.

LUKE 12–17; JOHN 11

Rejoice with Me; for I Have Found My Sheep Which Was Lost

MAY 6–12

As you study each set of verses, use the boxes to record what you are learning. Record the spiritual impressions you receive, the doctrinal truths you find, questions that come to mind, specific things you would like to teach your family, favorite phrases, etc. You can write, draw pictures, make diagrams... There is no right or wrong way.

*** NOTE: LUKE 13 WAS STUDIED ON PAGE 47, PLEASE REVIEW , OR ADD TO, YOUR NOTES ON THOSE PAGES.**

Christ instructs disciples **LUKE 12:1-7**	*Unpardonable sin* **LUKE 12:8-10**	*The Holy Ghost will tell you what to say* **LUKE 12:11-12**	*Parable of the Rich Fool* **LUKE 12:13-21**
Consider the lilies **LUKE 12:22-35**	*Prepare for the coming of the Lord* **LUKE 12:36-48**	*Preaching the gospel causes division* **LUKE 12:49-59**	*Christ heals on Sabbath* **LUKE 14:1-6**
Parable of the Wedding Guests **LUKE 14:7-11**	*Parable of the Great Supper* **LUKE 14:12-20**	*Parable of the Great Supper* **LUKE 14:21-24**	*Sacrifice required of all disciples* **LUKE 14:25-33**
Salt **LUKE 14:34-35**	*Pharisees and scribes murmur* **LUKE 15:1-3**	*Parable of the Lost Sheep* **LUKE 15:4-7**	*Parable of the Piece of Silver* **LUKE 15:8-10**
Parable of the Prodigal Son **LUKE 15:11-14**	*Parable of the Prodigal Son* **LUKE 15:15-19**	*Parable of the Prodigal Son* **LUKE 15:20-24**	*Parable of the Prodigal Son* **LUKE 15:25-32**

Parable of the Unjust Steward **LUKE 16:1-13**	*Divorce* **LUKE 16:14-18**	*Parable of Rich Man & Lazarus* **LUKE 16:19-23**	*Parable of Rich Man & Lazarus* **LUKE 16:24-31**
Offense and forgiveness **LUKE 17:1-4**	*Faith as a mustard seed* **LUKE 17:5-6**	*Parable of the Unprofitable Servant* **LUKE 17:7-10**	*The Ten Lepers* **LUKE 17:11-19**
The kingdom of God **LUKE 17:20-21**	*Apostasy and false Christs* **LUKE 17:22-25**	*When is the Second Coming?* **LUKE 17:26-30**	*Remember Lot's wife* **LUKE 17:31-33**
Some will abide the day **LUKE 17:34-37**	*Lazarus is sick* **JOHN 11:1-5**	*Lazarus had died* **JOHN 11:6-16**	*"Thy brother shall rise again"* **JOHN 11:17-27**
Jesus weeps **JOHN 11:28-36**	*Lazarus raised from the dead* **JOHN 11:37-46**	*Jewish leaders want Christ put to death* **JOHN 11:47-54**	*Jewish leaders try to locate Jesus* **JOHN 11:55-57**

May 6–12

Study these sections in *Come, Follow Me—For Individuals and Families: New Testament 2019*. As you study, record the teachings that stand out to you as well as any impressions you may receive. Be sure to make notes of any doctrines or principles you would like to discuss as a family in family home evening, family scripture study or in another setting.

1 *I should set my heart on eternally important things rather than on the things of this world.*

Luke 12; 14–16

2 *Heavenly Father rejoices when those who are lost are found.*

Luke 15

3 *What was Christ teaching in the parable of the unjust steward?*

Luke 16:1–12

4 *Gratitude for my blessings will bring me closer to God.*

Luke 17:11–19

5 *Jesus Christ is the Resurrection and the Life.*

John 11:1–46

FAMILY HOME EVENING • FAMILY SCRIPTURE STUDY

MAKE A PLAN

In the space below, make a plan on WHAT and HOW you would like to teach your family. As you plan, prayerfully consider each member of the family with their learning levels and personal needs. Also, consider how different family members can contribute to the teaching of the rest of the family. They could make visual aids, study a particular topic and prepare to teach the family, research something, etc.

TEACHING IDEAS FOR YOU:

- Before the lesson (even days before), hide something that your family will miss and you know they will spend some energy looking for (like the remote control, a toy, etc.). Lay out a robe, a pair of shoes (leather sandals if you have them), and a ring. Read the the Parable of the Prodigal Son in Luke 15:11-32 and/or watch the Bible Video on BibleVideos.org titled, "The Prodigal Son". On a poster board, make three columns and put "younger son" at the top of the first column, "father" at the top of the middle column, and "older son" at the top of the last column. In each column, write (or draw) what happened to each person, and include any lessons you learn from them. Talk about how important it was for the father's lost son to return, and then return the items you had hidden before the lesson. Ask everyone how they felt about their items being gone and how they feel about having them back again. Explain that these items are important to them, but replaceable, unlike the son of the father. Point to the robe, shoes, and ring and explain that the boy had been willing to return as his father's servant since he felt unworthy to return as his son, but the father immediately gave him items that were meant for his family. He was still his son. These are not things the servants would have. Testify of how much Heavenly Father loves each of them and share this quote by Elder Jeffrey R. Holland, "The tender image of this boy's anxious, faithful father running to meet him and showering him with kisses is one of the most moving and compassionate scenes in all of holy writ. It tells every child of God, wayward or otherwise, how much God wants us back in the protection of His arms" ("The Other Prodigal," Ensign, May 2002, 62). (Fun idea: Like the father had the "fatted calf" served at dinner, you could serve your family's favorite beef dish for dinner.)

MATTHEW 19–20; MARK 10; LUKE 18

What Lack I Yet?

MAY 13-19

As you study each set of verses, use the boxes to record what you are learning. Record the spiritual impressions you receive, the doctrinal truths you find, questions that come to mind, specific things you would like to teach your family, favorite phrases, etc. You can write, draw pictures, make diagrams... There is no right or wrong way.

Law of marriage and divorce **MATTHEW 19:1-12**	*Children will be saved* **MATTHEW 19:13-15**	*Importance of obedience* **MATTHEW 19:16-19**	*The rich young man* **MATTHEW 19:20-22**
Obedience and sacrifice **MATTHEW 19:23-30**	*Parable: Laborers in the Vineyard* **MATTHEW 20:1-4**	*Parable: Laborers in the Vineyard* **MATTHEW 20:5-8**	*Parable: Laborers in the Vineyard* **MATTHEW 20:9-12**
Parable: Laborers in the Vineyard **MATTHEW 20:13-16**	*Jesus foretells His death & resurrection* **MATTHEW 20:17-19**	*How to become great* **MATTHEW 20:20-28**	*Jesus heals blind men* **MATTHEW 20:29-34**
Marriage and divorce **MARK 10:1-12**	*Children shall be saved* **MARK 10:13-16**	*The rich young man* **MARK 10:17-20**	*The rich young man* **MARK 10:21-22**

Do not trust in riches **MARK 10:23-25**	*Who can be saved?* **MARK 10:26-27** * *Note the JST*	*Sacrifice all things* **MARK 10:28-31**	*Jesus foretells death & resurrection* **MARK 10:32-34**
How to be great **MARK 10:35-45**	*Jesus heals blind man* **MARK 10:46-52**	*Parable of the Unjust Judge* **LUKE 18:1-8**	*Parable of the Pharisee & Publican* **LUKE 18:9-12**
Parable of the Pharisee & Publican **LUKE 18:13-14**	*Children shall be saved* **LUKE 18:15-17**	*The rich young man* **LUKE 18:18-21**	*The rich young man* **LUKE 18:22-23**
Danger of riches **LUKE 18:24-27**	*Sacrifice* **LUKE 18:28-30**	*Jesus foretells death & resurrection* **LUKE 18:31-34**	*Jesus heals a blind man* **LUKE 18:35-43**

May 13-19

Study these sections in *Come, Follow Me—For Individuals and Families: New Testament 2019*. As you study, record the teachings that stand out to you as well as any impressions you may receive. Be sure to make notes of any doctrines or principles you would like to discuss as a family in family home evening, family scripture study or in another setting.

1 *Marriage between a man and a woman is ordained of God.*

Matthew 19:1–9; Mark 10:1–12

2 *Did Jesus teach that divorce is never acceptable or that divorced people should not remarry?*

Matthew 19:3–9; Mark 10:2–12

3 *If I ask the Lord, He will teach me what I need to do to inherit eternal life.*

Matthew 19:16–22; Mark 10:17–22; Luke 18:18–23

4 *Everyone can receive the blessing of eternal life, no matter when they accept the gospel.*

Matthew 20:1–16

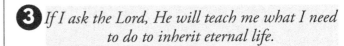

FAMILY HOME EVENING • FAMILY SCRIPTURE STUDY

MAKE A PLAN

In the space below, make a plan on WHAT and HOW you would like to teach your family. As you plan, prayerfully consider each member of the family with their learning levels and personal needs. Also, consider how different family members can contribute to the teaching of the rest of the family. They could make visual aids, study a particular topic and prepare to teach the family, research something, etc.

TEACHING IDEAS FOR YOU:

- Study Matthew 19:1-9 and Mark 10:1-12. Explain that the organization of the family has been important to Heavenly Father ever since Adam and Eve were put upon the earth. Give everyone a copy of "The Family: A Proclamation to the World" and lay out a stack of papers and markers. Have everyone select a phrase to illustrate and give everyone 5 minutes to draw it (tell them not to tell anyone what their phrase is). After 5 minutes, have everyone show their pictures while everyone guesses what phrase they were drawing (this is a good activity because they will be searching through "The Family: A Proclamation to the World" for the correct answers). Repeat this activity a second time, but this time have them illustrate a phrase they have a strong testimony of. Then repeat a third time and have them illustrate a phrase that they would like to understand better (this will be great information for you to know). Have everyone draw or write some of their favorite phrases in their own journals.

MATTHEW 21–23; MARK 11; LUKE 19–20; JOHN 12

Behold, Thy King Cometh

MAY 20–26

As you study each set of verses, use the boxes to record what you are learning. Record the spiritual impressions you receive, the doctrinal truths you find, questions that come to mind, specific things you would like to teach your family, favorite phrases, etc. You can write, draw pictures, make diagrams... There is no right or wrong way.

Triumphal entry **MATTHEW 21:1-11**	*Jesus cleanses the temple* **MATTHEW 21:12-17**	*Jesus curses fig tree* **MATTHEW 21:18-22**	*Jesus' authority* **MATTHEW 21:23-27**
Parable of the Two Sons **MATTHEW 21:28-32**	*Parable of the Wicked Husbandmen* **MATTHEW 21:33-46**	*Parable of the Marriage of King's Son* **MATTHEW 22:1-14**	*Render unto Caesar* **MATTHEW 22:15-22**
Law of eternal marriage **MATTHEW 22:23-33**	*Two great commandments* **MATTHEW 22:34-40**	*What think ye of Christ?* **MATTHEW 22:41-46**	*Christ speaks to scribes and Pharisees* **MATTHEW 23:1-12**
Christ speaks to scribes and Pharisees **MATTHEW 23:13-22**	*Weightier matters* **MATTHEW 23:23-24**	*Hypocrisy* **MATTHEW 23:25-28**	*Do not reject any prophet* **MATTHEW 23:29-36**
O Jerusalem **MATTHEW 23:37-39**	*Triumphal entry* **MARK 11:1-11**	*Jesus curses fig tree* **MARK 11:12-14**	*Jesus cleanses the temple* **MARK 11:15-19**

The fig tree **MARK 11:20-24**	*How to pray* **MARK 11:25-26**	*Jews argue with Jesus* **MARK 11:27-33**	*Zacchaeus* **LUKE 19:1-10**
Parable of the Pounds **LUKE 19:11-27**	*Triumphal entry* **LUKE 19:28-35**	*Triumphal entry* **LUKE 19:36-40**	*Jesus weeps over Jerusalem* **LUKE 19:41-44**
Jesus cleanses the temple **LUKE 19:45-48**	*Chief priests challenge Jesus* **LUKE 20:1-8**	*Parable of the Wicked Husbandmen* **LUKE 20:9-19**	*Render unto Caesar* **LUKE 20:20-26**
Eternal law of marriage **LUKE 20:27-40**	*Beware of scribes* **LUKE 20:41-47**	*Mary anoints Christ's feet* **JOHN 12:1-8**	*Chief priests consult about Lazarus* **JOHN 12:9-11**
Triumphal entry **JOHN 12:12-19**	*Jesus teaches disciples* **JOHN 12:20-30**	*Jesus teaches disciples* **JOHN 12:31-40**	*Jesus teaches disciples* **JOHN 12:41-50**

Study these sections in *Come, Follow Me—For Individuals and Families: New Testament 2019*. As you study, record the teachings that stand out to you as well as any impressions you may receive. Be sure to make notes of any doctrines or principles you would like to discuss as a family in family home evening, family scripture study or in another setting.

1 *The Lord judges not by the outward appearance but by the desires of the heart.*

Matthew 23; Luke 19:1–10; 20:45–47

2 *Jesus Christ is my King.*

Matthew 21:1–11; Mark 11:1–11; Luke 19:29–44; John 12:12–16

3 *The two great commandments are to love God and love others as myself.*

Matthew 22:34–40

4 *What are phylacteries?*

Matthew 23:5

FAMILY HOME EVENING • FAMILY SCRIPTURE STUDY

MAKE A PLAN

In the space below, make a plan on WHAT and HOW you would like to teach your family. As you plan, prayerfully consider each member of the family with their learning levels and personal needs. Also, consider how different family members can contribute to the teaching of the rest of the family. They could make visual aids, study a particular topic and prepare to teach the family, research something, etc.

TEACHING IDEAS FOR YOU:

- Explain that at this point in the New Testament, it is five days before the Savior's crucifixion. Show the picture "Triumphal Entry" found in the Church's Gospel Art book. Invite everyone to study the picture and tell you what they see. Ask the following questions:
    - **What is Christ riding?** *A donkey* (Old testament kings commonly rode donkeys)
    - **What are people holding and waving in the air?** *Palm branches* (Waving of palm branches was done when an Israelite king was crowned)
    - **What are others putting on the ground?** *Cloaks* (Crowds had spread their cloaks upon the ground when the Old Testament king, Jehu, was anointed king of Israel)
    - **What do all of these symbols have in common?** *He is entering in as a king.*
    - **Why do you think this is a courageous, bold, yet dangerous thing to do?** *The Jewish leaders were looking for any reason to condemn Christ. Currently the Jews were under Roman rule, so ultimately their ruler was Caesar. The Romans allowed the Jews to have a Jewish king, but that king answered to the Romans. The Jewish king at the time was Herod. In order to keep the Jews in check, Caesar had a man named Pontius Pilate live in Jerusalem and watch over the Jews and keep them in line. If Christ were claiming to be king of the Jews, this would have been considered treason to the Romans. Although He was not the crowned king, He was the King of heaven and earth, the Creator of the Earth, the King of all kings.*
    - **What did the people shout as he was entering in? Read Matthew 21:1-11 to see what they were shouting.** *Hosanna* (Hosanna means "save us").
- Watch the following Bible Videos on BibleVideos.org (these will help your children understand the hardness of the hearts of those who put Christ to death. Pause and talk about each video, and invite everyone to write about what they are learning in their personal journals.
    - "The Lord's Triumphal Entry into Jerusalem"
    - "Christ's Authority is Questioned"
    - "Render unto Caesar and unto God"

JOSEPH SMITH—MATTHEW 1; MATTHEW 25; MARK 12–13; LUKE 21

The Son of Man Shall Come

MAY 27–JUNE 2

As you study each set of verses, use the boxes to record what you are learning. Record the spiritual impressions you receive, the doctrinal truths you find, questions that come to mind, specific things you would like to teach your family, favorite phrases, etc. You can write, draw pictures, make diagrams... There is no right or wrong way.

Christ will come again **JOSEPH SMITH-MATTHEW 1:1**	*The temple will be destroyed* **JOSEPH SMITH-MATTHEW 1:2-3**	*Signs of the Second Coming* **JOSEPH SMITH-MATTHEW 1:4-9**	*Signs of the Second Coming* **JOSEPH SMITH-MATTHEW 1:10-11**
Signs of the Second Coming **JOSEPH SMITH-MATTHEW 1:12-20**	*Signs of the Second Coming* **JOSEPH SMITH-MATTHEW 1:21-26**	*Signs of the Second Coming* **JOSEPH SMITH-MATTHEW 1:27-35**	*Signs of the Second Coming* **JOSEPH SMITH-MATTHEW 1:36-40**
Signs of the Second Coming **JOSEPH SMITH-MATTHEW 1:41-48**	*Signs of the Second Coming* **JOSEPH SMITH-MATTHEW 1:49-55**	*The Parable of the Ten Virgins* **MATTHEW 25:1-3**	*The Parable of the Ten Virgins* **MATTHEW 25:4-7**
The Parable of the Ten Virgins **MATTHEW 25:8-10**	*The Parable of the Ten Virgins* **MATTHEW 25:11-13**	*The Parable of the Talents* **MATTHEW 25:14-18**	*The Parable of the Talents* **MATTHEW 25:19-22**
The Parable of the Talents **MATTHEW 25:23-26**	*The Parable of the Talents* **MATTHEW 25:27-30**	*The Parable of the Sheep and Goats* **MATTHEW 25:31-33**	*The Parable of the Sheep and Goats* **MATTHEW 25:34-36**
The Parable of the Sheep and Goats **MATTHEW 25:37-40**	*The Parable of the Sheep and Goats* **MATTHEW 25:41-46**	*Parable of the Wicked Husbandmen* **MARK 12:1-6**	*Parable of the Wicked Husbandmen* **MARK 12:7-12**

Render unto Caesar **MARK 12:13-17**	*Law of eternal marriage* **MARK 12:18-27**	*The two great commandments* **MARK 12:28-34**	*"What think ye of Christ?"* **MARK 12:35-37**
Jesus condemns scribes and Pharisees **MARK 12:38-40**	*The Widow's Mite* **MARK 12:41-44**	*Jesus foretells of temple's destruction* **MARK 13:1-2**	*Signs of Second Coming* **MARK 13:3-10**
Signs of Second Coming **MARK 13:11-25**	*Christ will return* **MARK 13:26-27**	*Parable of the Fig Tree* **MARK 13:28-29**	*All things will be fulfilled* **MARK 13:30-31**
When will Christ come? **MARK 13:32**	*How to prepare for Second Coming* **MARK 13:33-37**	*The Widow's Mite* **LUKE 21:1-4**	*Future destruction of temple* **LUKE 21:5-6**
False Christs will come **LUKE 21:7-8**	*Signs of the Second Coming* **LUKE 21:9-11**	*Persecution of saints* **LUKE 21:12-19**	*Destruction of Jerusalem* **LUKE 21:20-24**
Signs of the Second Coming **LUKE 21:25-28**	*Parable of the Fig Tree* **LUKE 21:29-31**	*All things will be fulfilled* **LUKE 21:32-33**	*How to prepare for Second Coming* **LUKE 21:34-38**

May 27–June 2

Study these sections in *Come, Follow Me—For Individuals and Families: New Testament 2019.* As you study, record the teachings that stand out to you as well as any impressions you may receive. Be sure to make notes of any doctrines or principles you would like to discuss as a family in family home evening, family scripture study or in another setting.

1 *What is Joseph Smith—Matthew?*

Joseph Smith—Matthew

2 *Prophecies about the Savior's Second Coming can help me face the future with faith.*

Joseph Smith—Matthew 1:21–37; Mark 13:21–37; Luke 21:25–38

3 *I must always be ready for the Savior's Second Coming.*

Joseph Smith—Matthew 1:26–27, 38–55; Matthew 25:1–13; Luke 21:29–36

4 *Heavenly Father expects me to use His gifts wisely.*

Matthew 25:14–30

5 *When I serve others, I am serving God.*

Matthew 25:31–46

6 *Will marriages continue after the Resurrection?*

Mark 12:18–27

FAMILY HOME EVENING • FAMILY SCRIPTURE STUDY

MAKE A PLAN

In the space below, make a plan on WHAT and HOW you would like to teach your family. As you plan, prayerfully consider each member of the family with their learning levels and personal needs. Also, consider how different family members can contribute to the teaching of the rest of the family. They could make visual aids, study a particular topic and prepare to teach the family, research something, etc.

TEACHING IDEAS FOR YOU:

- To teach the signs of the Second Coming ask your children:

  How do you know it is going to rain?
  How do you know you might be getting sick?
  How do you know that Winter is coming?

Explain that the answers to the questions above are all "signs". A sign is an indicator that lets you know something is coming. Ask them: "If you do not know the signs of Winter, does that mean Winter won't come?" (It will still come, but you might not be prepared.)
Ask the children if they know what the Second Coming is, and if they do not, explain it to them (*True to the Faith* has a great description.) Tell them the Second Coming has been spoken of for thousands of years, and the Lord has promised that there will be signs so that we can be prepared. Set out a stack of paper and markers. Together, study Joseph Smith- Matthew and whenever you come across one of the signs of the Second Coming, have your children draw that sign on a piece of paper. Also, encourage them to keep a list of signs in their journals. After you have all the signs drawn, put all the papers in a stack and flip them over so no one can see them. Take turns selecting a sign and describing it to everyone as they try to guess which sign you have.

- To teach how to be prepared at the Second Coming, set out any items you and your family have that show what you are doing to be prepared (gather items that show how you are trying to be temporally prepared as well as spiritually prepared). Read Luke 21:34-36 and talk about the importance of being prepared. Have the children guess how each item you set out helps your family be prepared for the Second Coming. Invite them to take 5 minutes and go to their rooms to find things that represent what they are doing to be prepared. Read the Parable of the Ten Virgins together in Matthew 25:1-13. Explain that this is a parable about girls who were ready when the bridegroom came, and it is symbolic of us being ready at the Second Coming. In this parable the virgins represent members of the Church, and the bridegroom represents Christ. The Lord explained to Joseph Smith that the wise virgins are those who "have received the truth, and have taken the Holy Spirit for their guide, and have not been deceived" (D&C 45:57). Watch the video called, "They that are Wise" (found on the LDS Media Library). Have your children cut out "drops" of oil from pieces of paper, and give each person a jar. Explain that throughout the week you are going to focus on being "wise" and every time they do something that helps them be prepared, they can add a drop of oil to their jar. Encourage them to keep a list in their personal journals of everything they do to earn a drop.

JOHN 13-17

Continue Ye in My Love

JUNE 3–9

As you study each set of verses, use the boxes to record what you are learning. Record the spiritual impressions you receive, the doctrinal truths you find, questions that come to mind, specific things you would like to teach your family, favorite phrases, etc. You can write, draw pictures, make diagrams... There is no right or wrong way.

Christ washes the feet of the Twelve **JOHN 13:1-20**	*Jesus speaks of Judas betraying him* **JOHN 13:21-30**
Love one another **JOHN 13:31-35**	*Jesus tells Peter that he will deny Him three times* **JOHN 13:36-38**
Jesus teaches of many mansions **JOHN 14:1-6**	*Those who have seen Christ have seen the Father* **JOHN 14:7-11**
Disciples will perform great miracles **JOHN 14:12-14**	*We show our love by keeping the commandments* **JOHN 14:15**

First and second Comforters **JOHN 14:16-31**	*Christ is the Vine* **JOHN 15:1-8**	*The perfect law of love* **JOHN 15:9-17**
The world will fight and hate true religion **JOHN 15:18-25**	*The Spirit will testify of Christ* **JOHN 15:26-27**	*What the world will do to Christ's servants* **JOHN 16:1-4**
The mission of the Holy Ghost **JOHN 16:5-15**	*Jesus teaches of Himself and what is coming* **JOHN 16:16-33**	*The great intercessory prayer* **JOHN 17:1**
Eternal life **JOHN 17:2-5**	*Jesus prays for His disciples* **JOHN 17:6-19**	*How the Father and the Son are one* **JOHN 17:20-26**

Study these sections in *Come, Follow Me—For Individuals and Families: New Testament 2019*. As you study, record the teachings that stand out to you as well as any impressions you may receive. Be sure to make notes of any doctrines or principles you would like to discuss as a family in family home evening, family scripture study or in another setting.

1 *I show my love for Jesus Christ by keeping His commandment to love.*

John 13–15

2 *The Holy Ghost helps me fulfill my purpose as a disciple of Jesus Christ.*

John 14–16

3 *As I abide in Christ, I will bring forth good fruit.*

John 15:1–8

4 *Jesus Christ intercedes for His disciples.*

John 17

5 *How are Jesus Christ and Heavenly Father one?*

John 17:11, 21–23

FAMILY HOME EVENING • FAMILY SCRIPTURE STUDY

MAKE A PLAN

In the space below, make a plan on WHAT and HOW you would like to teach your family. As you plan, prayerfully consider each member of the family with their learning levels and personal needs. Also, consider how different family members can contribute to the teaching of the rest of the family. They could make visual aids, study a particular topic and prepare to teach the family, research something, etc.

TEACHING IDEAS FOR YOU:

- Put out a plate with a cluster of grapes along with some other fruits. Ask your family what fruit came from a ______ tree (or plant). For example, if you have some strawberries, ask what fruit came from a strawberry plant. The point is to show that a plant can only produce a certain kind of fruit. A strawberry plant will never produce oranges. Show everyone what a grape vine looks like and have them draw the main vine in their journals and then draw some branches shooting off with leaves and grapes coming from the branches. Together read John 15:1-8 and label their vines with the teachings in these verses (so they will label the main vine as Christ and then the branches as different members of the family). Explain that "fruit" in verse 4 means the consequences that come from being connected with Christ. Discuss what these scriptures mean, and then have everyone make a list in their journals about the "fruits" they will have if they are connected to Christ.

- Read John 13:34-35 together. Ask: "How can someone tell if you and I are disciples of Christ?" (we love one another). Invite everyone to share a time that they felt truly loved by someone in the family. Now invite everyone to share a time they did something to show love for someone in the family. In journals, have everyone write down 3 things they will do that week to show love to members of the family. Have everyone share about their experiences at the end of the week.

MATTHEW 26; MARK 14; LUKE 22; JOHN 18

Not as I Will, but as Thou Wilt

JUNE 10-16

As you study each set of verses, use the boxes to record what you are learning. Record the spiritual impressions you receive, the doctrinal truths you find, questions that come to mind, specific things you would like to teach your family, favorite phrases, etc. You can write, draw pictures, make diagrams... There is no right or wrong way.

Jesus foretells of betrayal & crucifixion **MATTHEW 26:1-5**	*Mary anoints Jesus* **MATTHEW 26:6-13**	*Judas goes to chief priests* **MATTHEW 26:14-16**	*Passover meal arranged* **MATTHEW 26:17-20**
Jesus names Judas as betrayer **MATTHEW 26:21-25**	*The Sacrament* **MATTHEW 26:26-30**	*Peter declares his loyalty* **MATTHEW 26:31-35**	*Gethsemane* **MATTHEW 26:36-46**
Betrayal and arrest **MATTHEW 26:47-56**	*Jesus examined before Pilate* **MATTHEW 26:57-68**	*Peter denies knowing Christ* **MATTHEW 26:69-75**	*Jesus foretells of betrayal & crucifixion* **MARK 14:1-2**
Mary anoints Jesus **MARK 14:3-9**	*Judas arranges to betray Jesus* **MARK 14:10-11**	*Disciples arrange for Passover* **MARK 14:12-17**	*Jesus names Judas as His betrayer* **MARK 14:18-21**
The Sacrament **MARK 14:22-26**	*Apostles declare loyalty* **MARK 14:27-31**	*Gethsemane* **MARK 14:32-42**	*Jesus betrayed and arrested* **MARK 14:43-52**

Jesus examined before Caiaphas **MARK 14:53-65**	*Peter denies Christ* **MARK 14:66-72**	*Judas arranges to betray Jesus* **LUKE 22:1-6**	*Disciples arrange Passover meal* **LUKE 22:7-14**
The Sacrament **LUKE 22:15-20**	*Jesus says He will be betrayed* **LUKE 22:21-23**	*Who is the greatest among you?* **LUKE 22:24-30**	*Christ tells Peter he will deny Him* **LUKE 22:31-38**
Gethsemane **LUKE 22:39-46**	*Jesus betrayed and arrested* **LUKE 22:47-53**	*Peter denies Christ* **LUKE 22:54-62**	*Jesus is mocked, smitten, and tried* **LUKE 22:63-71**
Christ in Gethsemane **JOHN 18:1-2**	*Betrayal and arrest* **JOHN 18:3-11**	*Jesus taken to Annas* **JOHN 18:12-14**	*Peter denies Christ* **JOHN 18:15-18**
Jesus struck and examined **JOHN 18:19-23**	*Christ taken to Caiaphas* **JOHN 18:24**	*Peter denies Christ* **JOHN 18:25-27**	*Jesus examined by Pilate* **JOHN 18:28-40**

Study these sections in *Come, Follow Me—For Individuals and Families: New Testament 2019.* As you study, record the teachings that stand out to you as well as any impressions you may receive. Be sure to make notes of any doctrines or principles you would like to discuss as a family in family home evening, family scripture study or in another setting.

1 *The sacrament is an opportunity to remember the Savior.*

Matthew 26:17–30; Mark 14:12–26; Luke 22:7–39

2 *The Savior suffered for me in Gethsemane.*

Matthew 26:36–46; Mark 14:32–42; Luke 22:40–46

3 *Conversion is an ongoing process.*

Mark 14:27–31, 66–72; Luke 22:31–32

FAMILY HOME EVENING • FAMILY SCRIPTURE STUDY

MAKE A PLAN

In the space below, make a plan on WHAT and HOW you would like to teach your family. As you plan, prayerfully consider each member of the family with their learning levels and personal needs. Also, consider how different family members can contribute to the teaching of the rest of the family. They could make visual aids, study a particular topic and prepare to teach the family, research something, etc.

TEACHING IDEAS FOR YOU:

- Before the lesson, create a picture timeline by finding pictures online of the following events:
    - The Last Supper (Matthew 26:17–30; Mark 14:12–26; Luke 22:7–23, 39; John 13:1, 23–35; 14–17)
    - Gethsemane (Matthew 26:36–45; Luke 22:39–46, John 18: 1-2)
    - The Betrayal of Jesus (Matthew 26:14–16, 46–50; Mark 14:42–46; Luke 22:47–48; John 18:3–8, 12)
    - Jesus is mocked and tried (Matthew 26:57-68; Mark 14:53-65; Luke 22:63-71; John 18:19-24, 28-40)
    - Peter denying Christ (Matthew 26:69-75; Mark 14:66-72; Luke 22:54-62; John 18:25-27)

Read about each picture and have your children draw (or write) specific things that happened during each event and lay them around the pictures. After you have finished, gather their pictures, mix them up, and have them place them on the proper events again. Together, watch the Bible Videos on BibleVideos.org titled, "The Savior Suffers in Gethsemane," and "Jesus is Tried by Caiaphas, Peter Denies Knowing Him." Have everyone write what they learned about this special and sacred night in their personal journals.

- Consider having a dinner or snack that resembles the types of food Christ might have eaten during the Last Supper (it would have been a Passover, but following the symbolic dishes there would have been a feast). Some items might be: grape juice, pita bread, grapes, olives, lamb, fruits, vegetables, dates, nuts, etc. Lay it out with a tablecloth and candles to make it special and memorable.

MATTHEW 27; MARK 15; LUKE 23; JOHN 19

It is Finished

JUNE 17-23

As you study each set of verses, use the boxes to record what you are learning. Record the spiritual impressions you receive, the doctrinal truths you find, questions that come to mind, specific things you would like to teach your family, favorite phrases, etc. You can write, draw pictures, make diagrams... There is no right or wrong way.

Jesus tried and condemned **MATTHEW 27:1-2**	*Judas' death* **MATTHEW 27:3-10**	*Jesus tried before Pilate* **MATTHEW 27:11-18**	*Jesus tried before Pilate* **MATTHEW 27:19-23**
Jesus sentenced and mocked **MATTHEW 27:24-30**	*Jesus taken to Golgotha* **MATTHEW 27:31-38**	*Jesus mocked and scorned* **MATTHEW 27:39-43**	*Jesus on the cross* **MATTHEW 27:44-49**
Jesus' death **MATTHEW 27:50**	*Earth and man testify* **MATTHEW 27:51-54**	*Garden tomb* **MATTHEW 27:55-61**	*Pilate secures the tomb* **MATTHEW 27:62-66**
Jesus tried before Pilate **MARK 15:1-8**	*Jesus tried before Pilate* **MARK 15:9-14**	*Barabbas released* **MARK 15:15-19**	*Jesus taken to Golgotha* **MARK 15:20-23**
Jesus is put on the cross **MARK 15:24-28**	*Jesus mocked and scorned* **MARK 15:29-32**	*On the cross* **MARK 15:33-36**	*Jesus' death* **MARK 15:37-38**

Centurion testifies of Christ **MARK 15:39**	*Friends weep* **MARK 15:40-41**	*Jesus' body claimed and buried* **MARK 15:42-47**	*Jesus examined before Pilate* **LUKE 23:1-5**
Jesus examined by Herod **LUKE 23:6-12**	*Jesus again taken before Pilate* **LUKE 23:13-25**	*Jesus taken to Golgotha / put on cross* **LUKE 23:26-38**	*The two thieves* **LUKE 23:39-43**
Jesus' death **LUKE 23:44-46**	*Centurion testifies* **LUKE 23:47**	*Friends weep* **LUKE 23:48-49**	*Garden tomb* **LUKE 23:50-56**
Jesus before Pilate **JOHN 19:1-7**	*Jesus before Pilate* **JOHN 19:8-16**	*Jesus taken to Golgotha* **JOHN 19:17-22**	*Soldiers cast lots* **JOHN 19:23-24**
Jesus tells John to take care of Mary **JOHN 19:25-27**	*Christ on cross / death* **JOHN 19:28-30**	*Christ's side pierced and legs broken* **JOHN 19:31-37**	*Christ's body claimed and put in tomb* **JOHN 19:38-42**

Study these sections in *Come, Follow Me—For Individuals and Families: New Testament 2019*. As you study, record the teachings that stand out to you as well as any impressions you may receive. Be sure to make notes of any doctrines or principles you would like to discuss as a family in family home evening, family scripture study or in another setting.

1 *Jesus Christ's willingness to suffer shows His love for the Father and for all of us.*

Matthew 27; Mark 15; Luke 23; John 19

2 *Mocking of God's truth should not weaken my faith.*

Matthew 27:27–49, 54; Mark 15:16–32; Luke 23:11, 35–39; John 19:1–5

3 *Did Heavenly Father forsake Jesus on the cross?*

Matthew 27:46; Mark 15:34

4 *The Savior is our example of forgiveness.*

Luke 23:34

5 *What is the meaning of "paradise" in the Savior's statement to the thief?*

Luke 23:39–43

FAMILY HOME EVENING • FAMILY SCRIPTURE STUDY

MAKE A PLAN

In the space below, make a plan on WHAT and HOW you would like to teach your family. As you plan, prayerfully consider each member of the family with their learning levels and personal needs. Also, consider how different family members can contribute to the teaching of the rest of the family. They could make visual aids, study a particular topic and prepare to teach the family, research something, etc.

TEACHING IDEAS FOR YOU:

- Create your own timeline of the events from the trials and crucifixion of Jesus by gathering 12 pieces of paper. On the top of each paper, write the following captions and scripture references (the first 3 are from last week's study and are good for review and context). *Tip: Put bookmarks in your scriptures in Matthew 26, Mark 14, Luke 22, and John 13 so you can easily flip back and forth.

1- **The Last Supper** (Matthew 26:20-30; Mark 14:17-26; Luke 22:14-38; John 13:21-30)
2- **The Garden of Gethsemane** (Matthew 26:36-46; Mark 14:32-42; Luke 22:39-45)
3- **Jesus is betrayed and arrested** (Matthew 26:47-56; Mark 14:43-52; Luke 22:47-53; John 18:1-11)
4- **Jewish religious leaders condemn Jesus** (Matthew 27:1-2; Mark 15:1; Luke 22:66-71)
5- **Jesus is sent to Pilate** (the Roman Governor over Israel) (Matthew 27:11-14; Mark 15:2-5; Luke 23:1-5; John 18:28-37)
* The religious leaders could not legally put Jesus to death; only the Roman leaders could give such a sentence, so the religous leaders sent Jesus to Pilate who found him innocent, and then sent him to Herod (the Jewish king).
6- **Jesus is sent to Herod** (Luke 23:6-12)
7- **Jesus is sent back to Pilate** (Luke 23:11)
8- **Jesus is sentenced to death** (Matthew 27:26; Mark 15:15; Luke 23:23-24; John 19:16)
9- **Jesus taken to Golgotha** (Matthew 27:32-34; Mark 15:21-24; Luke 23:26-31; John 19:16-17)
10- **The Crucifixion** (Matthew 27:35-50; Mark 15:24-38; Luke 23:33-46; John 19:18-37)
11- **At death** (Matthew 27:51-54; Mark 15:39-41; Luke 23:47-49)
12- **Jesus' burial** (Matthew 27:55-56; Mark 15:42-47; Luke 23:50-56; John 19:38-42)

As a family, go through each page together and fill in the pages with details about each event. You can draw pictures, make diagrams, write phrases that were said, write insights or questions you have, quote a family member's words about that event, quotes from prophets and apostles, etc. You could also print pictures from the internet that show what different things might have looked like and glue them to the pages (for example you could print a picture of Golgotha, or a picture of what Pilate might have looked like). You could also have your children add some art to the timeline by making a watercolor painting of the Garden Tomb for #12 (Jesus' burial) or an olive tree for #2. Once you have completed the timeline, have everyone record the timeline in their journals, or draw some signifcant events in their journals. Then together, watch the Bible Videos on BibleVideos.org called, "Jesus is Condemned Before Pilate," "Jesus is Scourged and Crucified," and "Jesus is Laid in a Tomb."

*NOTE: Save timeline for next week's activity (see page 101).

MATTHEW 28; MARK 16; LUKE 24; JOHN 20–21

He Is Risen

JUNE 24-30

As you study each set of verses, use the boxes to record what you are learning. Record the spiritual impressions you receive, the doctrinal truths you find, questions that come to mind, specific things you would like to teach your family, favorite phrases, etc. You can write, draw pictures, make diagrams... There is no right or wrong way.

Mary Magdalene finds empty tomb **MATTHEW 28:1-7**	*Jesus appears to women* **MATTHEW 28:8-10**	*Chief Priests learn of Jesus' resurrection* **MATTHEW 28:11-15**	*Jesus appears to disciples in Galilee* **MATTHEW 28:16-20**
Mary Magdalene finds empty tomb **MARK 16:1-8**	*Jesus appears to Mary Magdalene* **MARK 16:9-11**	*Road to Emmaus* **MARK 16:12-13**	*Jesus appears to Apostles* **MARK 16:14**
Jesus appears to disciples in Galilee **MARK 16:15-18**	*Jesus ascends to Heaven* **MARK 16:19-20**	*Women and Peter find empty tomb* **LUKE 24:1-12**	*Road to Emmaus* **LUKE 24:13-16**
Road to Emmaus **LUKE 24:17-24**	*Road to Emmaus* **LUKE 24:25-29**	*Road to Emmaus* **LUKE 24:30-32**	*Christ appears to Peter* **LUKE 24:33-35**

Christ appears to disciples **LUKE 24:36-44**	*Ye are witnesses* **LUKE 24:45-49**	*Jesus ascends to Heaven* **LUKE 24:50-53**	*Mary Magdalene finds empty tomb* **JOHN 20:1-2**
Peter and John find empty tomb **JOHN 20:3-10**	*Jesus appears to Mary Magdalene* **JOHN 20:11-18**	*Jesus appears to Apostles* **JOHN 20:19-21**	*Apostles receive Holy Ghost* **JOHN 20:22-23**
Thomas **JOHN 20:24-29**	*Purpose of John's book* **JOHN 20:30-31**	*Disciples go fishing* **JOHN 21:1-4**	*Resurrected Christ appears to them* **JOHN 21:5-8**
Christ on shore **JOHN 21:9-14**	*Feed my sheep* **JOHN 21:15-17**	*Peter will be a martyr / John will be translated* **JOHN 21:18-24**	*What Christ did* **JOHN 21:25**

Study these sections in *Come, Follow Me—For Individuals and Families: New Testament 2019*. As you study, record the teachings that stand out to you as well as any impressions you may receive. Be sure to make notes of any doctrines or principles you would like to discuss as a family in family home evening, family scripture study or in another setting.

1 *Because Jesus was resurrected, I too will be resurrected.*

Matthew 28; Mark 16; Luke 24; John 20

2 *We can invite the Savior to "abide with us."*

Luke 24:13–35

3 *Does Jesus Christ have a body?*

Luke 24:36–43; John 20

4 *"Blessed are they that have not seen, and yet have believed."*

John 20:19–29

5 *The Savior invites me to feed His sheep.*

John 21:1–17

FAMILY HOME EVENING • FAMILY SCRIPTURE STUDY

MAKE A PLAN

In the space below, make a plan on WHAT and HOW you would like to teach your family. As you plan, prayerfully consider each member of the family with their learning levels and personal needs. Also, consider how different family members can contribute to the teaching of the rest of the family. They could make visual aids, study a particular topic and prepare to teach the family, research something, etc.

TEACHING IDEAS FOR YOU:

- Take out your timeline from last week's teaching idea and review all the events from the Atonement through the Crucifixion. Explain that the timeline ended in a very sad way, but today you are going to add to it in a way that will cause us to rejoice forever. Gather 6 more pieces of paper to add to your timeline the following captions and scripture references:

1. **Resurrected Jesus appears to Mary Magdalene** (Mark 16:1-11; John 20:11-18)
2. **Resurrected Jesus appears to women** (Matthew 28:8-10)
3. **Resurrected Jesus appears to Apostles** (Matthew 28:16-20; Mark 16:14-18; Luke 24:33-49; John 20:19-21)
4. **Resurrected Jesus appears to Thomas** (John 20:24-29)
5. **The Road to Emmaus** (Mark 16:12-13; Luke 24:13-32)
6. **Jesus tells Apostles to "Feed My Sheep"** (John 21:1-17)

As a family, go through each page together and fill in the pages with details about each event. You can draw pictures, make diagrams, write phrases that were said, write insights or questions you have, quote a family member's words about that event, quotes from prophets and apostles, etc. You could also print pictures from the internet that show what different things might have looked like and glue them to the pages (for example, you could print a picture of the Garden Tomb). You could also have your children add some art to the timeline by making a watercolor painting of the Road to Emmaus or the Apostles fishing on the Sea of Galilee.

Once you have completed the timeline, have everyone record the timeline in their journals, or draw some signifcant events in their journals. Then together, watch the Bible Videos on BibleVideos.org called:

1- "Jesus is Resurrected"
2- "My Kingdom is Not of This World"
3- "He is Risen"
4- "Christ Appears on the Road to Emmaus"
5- " The Risen Lord Appears to the Apostles"
6- "Blessed Are They That Have Not Seen, and Yet Have Believed"
7- "Feed My Sheep."

ACTS 1–5

Ye Shall Be Witnesses unto Me

JULY 1–7

As you study each set of verses, use the boxes to record what you are learning. Record the spiritual impressions you receive, the doctrinal truths you find, questions that come to mind, specific things you would like to teach your family, favorite phrases, etc. You can write, draw pictures, make diagrams... There is no right or wrong way.

Apostles told to wait for Holy Ghost **ACTS 1:1-5**	*Apostles will be witnesses* **ACTS 1:6-8**	*Christ ascends to Heaven* **ACTS 1:9-14**	*New Apostle to replace Judas* **ACTS 1:15-26**
Day of Pentecost **ACTS 2:1-5**	*Gift of tongues* **ACTS 2:6-11**	*Some amazed / Others mock* **ACTS 2:12-13**	*Peter quotes Joel* **ACTS 2:14-21**
Peter testifies of Christ's resurrection **ACTS 2:22-36**	*Peter teaches how to be saved* **ACTS 2:37-40**	*3,000 people baptized* **ACTS 2:41-47**	*Peter heals lame man at temple* **ACTS 3:1-8**
Everyone amazed **ACTS 3:9-11**	*Peter healed through Christ's power* **ACTS 3:12**	*Peter boldly testifies of Christ* **ACTS 3:13-18**	*Moses taught about Christ* **ACTS 3:19-26**

Jewish leaders arrest Peter **ACTS 4:1-3**	*Peter testifies to same leaders who had Christ put to death* **ACTS 4:4-8**	*Peter testifies to same leaders who had Christ put to death* **ACTS 4:9-12**	*Leaders seek to silence Peter and John* **ACTS 4:13-17**
Peter and John must testify **ACTS 4:18-22**	*Peter and John report* **ACTS 4:23-31**	*Saints live United Order* **ACTS 4:32-34**	*Saints live United Order* **ACTS 4:35-37**
Ananias and Sapphira **ACTS 5:1-11**	*Many signs, wonders, and miracles* **ACTS 5:12-16**	*Apostles imprisoned* **ACTS 5:17-18**	*Angel delivers them from prison* **ACTS 5:19-20**
Apostles teach in temple **ACTS 5:21-25**	*Apostles questioned by Jewish leaders* **ACTS 5:26-32**	*Gamaliel* **ACTS 5:33-40**	*Apostles do not stop preaching* **ACTS 5:41-42**

Study these sections in *Come, Follow Me—For Individuals and Families: New Testament 2019.* As you study, record the teachings that stand out to you as well as any impressions you may receive. Be sure to make notes of any doctrines or principles you would like to discuss as a family in family home evening, family scripture study or in another setting.

1 *Jesus Christ directs His Church through the Holy Ghost.*

Acts 1:1–8, 15–26; 2:1–42; 4:1–13, 31–33

2 *What is the purpose of the gift of tongues?*

Acts 2:1–18

3 *The first principles and ordinances of the gospel help me come unto Christ.*

Acts 2:36–47; 3:13–21

4 *What are "the times of refreshing" and "the times of restitution of all things"?*

Acts 3:19–21

5 *Disciples of Jesus Christ are given power to perform miracles in His name.*

Acts 3; 4:1–31; 5:12–42

FAMILY HOME EVENING • FAMILY SCRIPTURE STUDY

MAKE A PLAN

In the space below, make a plan on WHAT and HOW you would like to teach your family. As you plan, prayerfully consider each member of the family with their learning levels and personal needs. Also, consider how different family members can contribute to the teaching of the rest of the family. They could make visual aids, study a particular topic and prepare to teach the family, research something, etc.

TEACHING IDEAS FOR YOU:

- Get a peanut in a shell (or some other kind of nut), and hold it in your hands so that no one can see what you are holding. Tell your family that you are holding something that no one has ever seen or touched before, not even you (you are holding the shell, not the peanut). Ask everyone if they believe you (your family might doubt you and will want to see for themselves). Call up someone to be a witness and have them peek into your hands and (without telling everyone what you are holding) have them confirm that you are indeed holding something that no one has ever seen or held before. Ask them if they believe you now that there are two witnesses. Have everyone open up to Acts 1:1-11 and read what the Lord told the Apostles they would now be. Just like (now show them the peanut) you knew what you were saying was true, these Apostles had seen the resurrected Lord and now were to be special witnesses of Him to the rest of the world. Explain that there are special witnesses that live today. Find a picture online of the Quorum of the 12 Apostles and First Presidency and print one for each family member. Make a booklet for each person by stapling 15 sheets of paper to the picture, or use a report cover to attach the pages together. Challenge your children to come to know more about these special witnesses and create a book about them. On the top of each sheet of paper, write one Church leader's name. For example, the prophet's name will be on one sheet, the first counselor on another sheet, the second counselor on another sheet, and so on until there is a page for each member of the First Presidency and Quorum of the Twelve. Divide the leaders up among your family and have them learn about them and their lives. They can keep notes on their pages by writing, drawing, or printing pictures from online and gluing them onto their page. Throughout the week have everyone give reports on their assigned leader while everyone takes notes in their own booklets.
- On a poster board (and in personal journals) make two columns and write "Peter Before" on the left side, and "Peter After" on the right side. On the left side, review the scriptures when Peter denied Christ (Matthew 26:69-75; Mark 14:66-72; Luke 22:54-62; and John 18:25-27) and write what happened in the column. On the right side, read Acts 3 and after every few verses draw or write what Peter did. Point out the courage that Peter now has. After healing a lame man at the crowded temple, he then stood before the very men who plotted to have Jesus killed, and he testified with boldness. Ask your children why they think Peter has changed so much (possible answers are that he now has the Gift of the Holy Ghost, he was told to be a witness, and he is now the president of the Church). Have your children each come up to the poster board and write something they have learned from this story. You could also think of several scenarios your children might encounter at school or with friends where it would take courage to do the right thing. Talk through each scenario and how your children could be like Peter in the "after" column (strong, bold, and courageous).

*Note: There are four Bible Videos on BibleVideos.org that teach the stories in these chapters.

ACTS 6–9

What Wilt Thou Have Me to Do?

JULY 8-14

As you study each set of verses, use the boxes to record what you are learning. Record the spiritual impressions you receive, the doctrinal truths you find, questions that come to mind, specific things you would like to teach your family, favorite phrases, etc. You can write, draw pictures, make diagrams... There is no right or wrong way.

Apostles choose 7 to assist them **ACTS 6:1-6**	*Stephen did great miracles* **ACTS 6:7-8**	*Stephen tried before Sanhedrin* **ACTS 6:9-14**	*Stephen transfigured* **ACTS 6:15**
Stephen testifies before Sanhedrin **ACTS 7:1-8**	*Stephen testifies before Sanhedrin* **ACTS 7:9-16**	*Stephen testifies before Sanhedrin* **ACTS 7:17-29**	*Stephen testifies before Sanhedrin* **ACTS 7:30-36**
Stephen testifies before Sanhedrin **ACTS 7:37-47**	*Stephen testifies before Sanhedrin* **ACTS 7:48-53**	*Sanhedrin is angry* **ACTS 7:54**	*Stephen sees Father and Son* **ACTS 7:55-56**
Stephen stoned **ACTS 7:57-60**	*Saul persecutes the Church* **ACTS 8:1-4**	*Philip ministers in Samaria / Simon* **ACTS 8:5-13**	*Apostles come to Samaria* **ACTS 8:14-17**
Simon tries to buy gift of the Holy Ghost **ACTS 8:18-25**	*Philip preaches in Jerusalem* **ACTS 8:26-34**	*Philip preaches in Jerusalem* **ACTS 8:35-40**	*Saul persecutes the Church* **ACTS 9:1-2**

Jesus appears to Saul **ACTS 9:3-6**	*Saul blinded* **ACTS 9:7-9**	*The Lord tells Ananias to go to Saul* **ACTS 9:10-13**
The Lord tells Ananias to go to Saul **ACTS 9:14-16**	*Ananias restores Saul's sight* **ACTS 9:17-19**	*Saul begins to preach of Christ* **ACTS 9:20-22**
Jews sought to kill Christ **ACTS 9:23-25**	*Disciples afraid of Saul* **ACTS 9:26-27**	*Saul taught with disciples* **ACTS 9:28-29**
Disciples protect Saul **ACTS 9:30-31**	*Peter raises Tabitha from the dead* **ACTS 9:32-38**	*Peter raises Tabitha from the dead* **ACTS 9:39-43**

Study these sections in *Come, Follow Me—For Individuals and Families: New Testament 2019*. As you study, record the teachings that stand out to you as well as any impressions you may receive. Be sure to make notes of any doctrines or principles you would like to discuss as a family in family home evening, family scripture study or in another setting.

1 *My heart needs to be "right in the sight of God."*

Acts 6–8

2 *Resisting the Holy Ghost can lead to rejecting the Savior and His prophets.*

Acts 6–7

3 *Besides Stephen, who else was martyred for their testimony of Jesus Christ?*

Acts 7:54–60

4 *The Holy Ghost will help me guide others to Jesus Christ.*

Acts 8:26–39

5 *When I submit to the Lord's will, I can become an instrument in His hands.*

Acts 9:1–31

FAMILY HOME EVENING • FAMILY SCRIPTURE STUDY

MAKE A PLAN

In the space below, make a plan on WHAT and HOW you would like to teach your family. As you plan, prayerfully consider each member of the family with their learning levels and personal needs. Also, consider how different family members can contribute to the teaching of the rest of the family. They could make visual aids, study a particular topic and prepare to teach the family, research something, etc.

TEACHING IDEAS FOR YOU:

- If you or someone in your family served a mission, lay out several items from your mission. Talk about those items with your family and share some of your missionary experiences. Talk about some things that you did to prepare for your mission and how doing those things made a difference on your mission. Invite your children to draw three pictures of men from the New Testament: a picture of Stephen, a picture of Philip, and a picture of Paul (known as Saul until Acts 13:9). After they draw the pictures, explain that these men were amazing missionaries and are great example to us on the kind of disciples we can be. Set out some sticky notes and read about each man (use your scripture boxes on pages 106 and 107 for references). As the children learn about them, have them identify things each man did, or characteristics they had, and draw or write them on the sticky notes and stick them on the picture of the man they are writing about. At the end, ask everyone to look over all of the sticky notes and choose one that has a quality they would like to possess. Have them describe the disciple they chose. Tell each person to take the sticky note they selected and put it up somewhere in their room or personal space. Challenge them to make an effort this week to gain the qualities on the sticky note they selected. Have everyone keep notes of their progress in their personal journals.

ACTS 10-15

The Word of God Grew and Multiplied

JULY 15–21

As you study each set of verses, use the boxes to record what you are learning. Record the spiritual impressions you receive, the doctrinal truths you find, questions that come to mind, specific things you would like to teach your family, favorite phrases, etc. You can write, draw pictures, make diagrams... There is no right or wrong way.

An angel ministers to Cornelius (a Roman officer) **ACTS 10:1-8**	*Peter's vision* **ACTS 10:9-14**	*Peter's vision* **ACTS 10:15-20**	*Peter and Cornelius meet* **ACTS 10:21-27**
Meaning of Peter's vision **ACTS 10:28**	*Gospel should go to every nation* **ACTS 10:29-35**	*We are witnesses* **ACTS 10:36-39**	*Commanded to preach and testify* **ACTS 10:40-43**
Holy Ghost given to Gentiles **ACTS 10:44-48**	*Gift of repentance given to Gentiles* **ACTS 11:1-18**	*Gospel taken to Jews and Gentiles* **ACTS 11:19-21**	*Barnabas* **ACTS 11:22-24**
Disciples called Christians **ACTS 11:25-26**	*The Spirit is guiding the work* **ACTS 11:27-30**	*James is put to death* **ACTS 12:1-2**	*Herod imprisons Peter* **ACTS 12:3-5**
An angel frees Peter from prison **ACTS 12:6-10**	*Peter takes refuge with other disciples* **ACTS 12:11-17**	*Herod's death* **ACTS 12:18-23**	*The word of God grew* **ACTS 12:24-25**

Saul and Barnabas called to missionary work **ACTS 13:1-3**	*They preach in Cyprus* **ACTS 13:4-5**	*Saul is now Paul* **ACTS 13:6-9**	*Paul curses sorcerer* **ACTS 13:10-12**
Paul preaches in synagogue in Antioch **ACTS 13:13-41**	*Many gather to hear word of God* **ACTS 13:42-44**	*Jews fuel envy* **ACTS 13:45-46**	*Word of the Lord throughout the land* **ACTS 13:47-49**
Persecution, yet joy **ACTS 13:50-52**	*Jews stir up Gentiles* **ACTS 14:1-7**	*Paul heals lame man* **ACTS 14:8-10**	*Paul & Barnabas thought to be Gods* **ACTS 14:11-18**
Paul stoned **ACTS 14:19-20**	*Paul continues preaching* **ACTS 14:21-28**	*Disputes concerning circumcision* **ACTS 15:1-3**	*Issue taken to Apostles* **ACTS 15:4-5**
Peter takes charge of issue **ACTS 15:6-21**	*Chosen men sent out to resolve questions* **ACTS 15:22-29**	*Antioch rejoices in answer* **ACTS 15:30-31**	*Paul & Barnabas continue preaching* **ACTS 15:32-41**

Acts 10–15

July 15-21

Study these sections in *Come, Follow Me—For Individuals and Families: New Testament 2019.* As you study, record the teachings that stand out to you as well as any impressions you may receive. Be sure to make notes of any doctrines or principles you would like to discuss as a family in family home evening, family scripture study or in another setting.

1 *"God is no respecter of persons."*

Acts 10

2 *Heavenly Father teaches me line upon line through revelation.*

Acts 10; 11:1–18; 15

3 *I am a Christian because I believe in and follow Jesus Christ.*

Acts 11:26

FAMILY HOME EVENING • FAMILY SCRIPTURE STUDY

MAKE A PLAN

In the space below, make a plan on WHAT and HOW you would like to teach your family. As you plan, prayerfully consider each member of the family with their learning levels and personal needs. Also, consider how different family members can contribute to the teaching of the rest of the family. They could make visual aids, study a particular topic and prepare to teach the family, research something, etc.

TEACHING IDEAS FOR YOU:

- Lay out a picnic blanket on your floor and set out several foreign foods. Invite your family to eat and try everything, especially if there are things they have not tried before (try to get some foods that are really strange). Put out a poster board and draw the following figures:

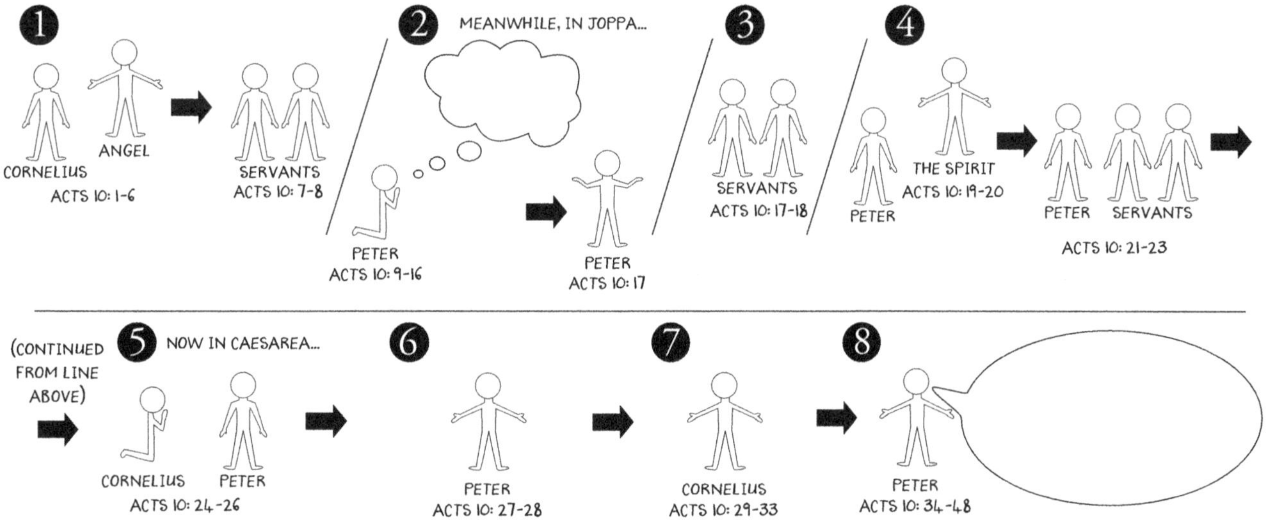

- Read the story with your family and have the children finish the pictures by adding proper clothing and other details as you read. Here are some tips for you:

Picture #1: Cornelius was leader in the Roman army. He was s centurion which means he was over 100 soldiers. He was a Gentile, and at this time the Gospel had not been taken to the Gentiles. The Jews considered them unclean, and the Jews that were now Christians still considered them unclean so they had only been baptizing Jews.

Picture #2: Peter is the President of the Church. If there were to be any policy changes (like who could be baptized) he would need to receive that revelation. So Peter had a vision. In the thought cloud, have your children draw the vision. The Jews were still keeping Jewish law, like what they could and could not eat. Under the law of Moses, Jews were forbidden to eat animals that were designated as common or unclean. The vision was of a great sheet full of different meats (meats that the jews considered unclean) that had previously been forbidden. Peter did not understand the meaning of the vision yet.

Picture #6: As Peter entered into the room that was full of Gentiles, he suddenly understood the meaning of the vision. No man (i.e. the Gentiles) should be considered unclean. Have the children draw Cornelius' friends and family.

Picture #8: Peter then teaches the Gentiles. Have the children draw or write some things that Peter taught and make sure to add where Peter commands them to be baptized (the first Gentile baptisms) in verse 48.

- Watch the Bible Video on BibleVideos.org titled, "Peter's Revelation to Take the Gospel to the Gentiles."

- Point out all of the foreign foods on the tablecloth. Explain that just as these foods seemed strange to you, they represent people living in other parts of the world, and they are Heavenly Father's children too. He loves them, just as He loves us.

- In your personal journals write, "God is no respecter of persons" (Acts 10:34) and write about what you have learned today.

ACTS 16–21

The Lord Had Called Us for to Preach the Gospel

JULY 22-28

As you study each set of verses, use the boxes to record what you are learning. Record the spiritual impressions you receive, the doctrinal truths you find, questions that come to mind, specific things you would like to teach your family, favorite phrases, etc. You can write, draw pictures, make diagrams... There is no right or wrong way.

Timotheus **ACTS 16:1-3**	*Churches established* **ACTS 16:4-5**	*The Spirit directs where gospel should be preached* **ACTS 16:6-11**	*Lydia* **ACTS 16:12-15**
Paul casts out evil spirit **ACTS 16:16-18**	*Paul & Silas beaten and imprisoned* **ACTS 16:19-24**	*Paul and Silas in prison* **ACTS 16:25**	*Prison shakes / Jailor converted* **ACTS 16:26-33**
Paul and Silas depart **ACTS 16:34-40**	*Paul and Silas preach in Thessalonica* **ACTS 17:1-4**	*Persecution stirred by Jews* **ACTS 17:5-9**	*Paul and Silas go to preach in Berea* **ACTS 17:10-12**
Persecutors follow them there **ACTS 17:13-14**	*Paul in Athens* **ACTS 17:15-21**	*Paul at Mars' Hill* **ACTS 17:22-23**	*Paul at Mars' Hill* **ACTS 17:24-28**
Paul at Mars' Hill **ACTS 17:29-34**	*Paul preaches in Corinth* **ACTS 18:1-11**	*Paul on trial* **ACTS 18:12-17**	*Paul travels / Apollos* **ACTS 18:18-28**

Disciples properly baptized **ACTS 19:1-7**	*Paul preaches in Asia* **ACTS 19:8-10**	*Special miracles* **ACTS 19:11-12**	*Seven sons cannot cast out evil spirit without Priesthood authority* **ACTS 19:13-20**
Pagan priests turn people against Paul **ACTS 19:21-26**	*Pagan priests turn people against Paul* **ACTS 19:27-33**	*Pagan priests turn people against Paul* **ACTS 19:34-41**	*Eutychus raised from dead* **ACTS 20:1-12**
Paul's travels **ACTS 20:13-17**	*Paul speaks with elders of church* **ACTS 20:18-28**	*Paul knows persecution lies ahead* **ACTS 20:29-32**	*Parting words* **ACTS 20:33-35**
Sorrowful farewell **ACTS 20:36-38**	*Paul told not to go to Jerusalem* **ACTS 21:1-4**	*Paul again told not to go to Jerusalem* **ACTS 21:5-12**	*Paul goes to Jerusalem* **ACTS 21:13-16**
Paul received by brethren **ACTS 21:17-26**	*Paul persecuted and beaten* **ACTS 21:27-32**	*Paul arrested and bound* **ACTS 21:33-36**	*Paul asks to speak to people* **ACTS 21:37-40**

Acts 16–21

July 22-28

Study these sections in *Come, Follow Me—For Individuals and Families: New Testament 2019.* As you study, record the teachings that stand out to you as well as any impressions you may receive. Be sure to make notes of any doctrines or principles you would like to discuss as a family in family home evening, family scripture study or in another setting.

1 *The Spirit will guide me in my efforts to share the gospel.*

Acts 16–21

2 *I can declare the gospel in all circumstances.*

Acts 16–21

3 *"We are the offspring of God."*

Acts 17:16–34

FAMILY HOME EVENING • FAMILY SCRIPTURE STUDY

MAKE A PLAN

In the space below, make a plan on WHAT and HOW you would like to teach your family. As you plan, prayerfully consider each member of the family with their learning levels and personal needs. Also, consider how different family members can contribute to the teaching of the rest of the family. They could make visual aids, study a particular topic and prepare to teach the family, research something, etc.

TEACHING IDEAS FOR YOU:

- Print the Bible Map titled "The Missionary Journeys of the Apostle Paul." As you and your children study these chapters, have them follow along the map and write or draw things that happened at each location.

- Acts 19:1-7 is a great place to teach your children about the importance of baptism by the proper authority. After you discuss the scripture story, have your children create a "book report" type visual about baptism. You could get a tri-fold foam core poster and tell them to study about baptism using the scriptures, *True to the Faith*, and any other resources you have. As they study instruct them to fill the poster with visuals that teach about baptism, and then when they are finished, have them present their report to you.

- Acts 17:16-34 is a wonderful place to teach your children about who Heavenly Father is. Your *Come, Follow Me—For Individuals and Families: New Testament 2019* manual has some great study tips for these verses. If you review those tips, you can decide how to discuss those verses with your family. Help your children understand that people all over the world and throughout time have had a lot of different views about who Heavenly Father is because they haven't seen Him. Talk about the First Vision and what Joseph Smith learned about Heavenly Father. In their journals, have them write the question, "What do I know about Heavenly Father?" and then study about Him using *True to the Faith: God the Father,* and encourage them to fill their journal page with descriptions and drawings of what they learned.

ACTS 22–28

A Minister and a Witness

JULY 29 - AUGUST 4

As you study each set of verses, use the boxes to record what you are learning. Record the spiritual impressions you receive, the doctrinal truths you find, questions that come to mind, specific things you would like to teach your family, favorite phrases, etc. You can write, draw pictures, make diagrams... There is no right or wrong way.

Paul tells about his conversion **ACTS 22:1-16**	*Another vision Paul had* **ACTS 22:17-21**	*People reject Paul's testimony* **ACTS 22:22-23**	*Paul is a Roman* **ACTS 22:24-30**
Paul before Ananias **ACTS 23:1-5**	*Pharisees & Sadducees contend* **ACTS 23:6-10**	*The Lord appears to Paul* **ACTS 23:11**	*Jews ready to kill Paul* **ACTS 23:12-15**
Paul's nephew **ACTS 23:16-22**	*Paul taken to Felix* **ACTS 23:23-27**	*Paul taken to Felix* **ACTS 23:28-31**	*Felix agrees to hear Paul* **ACTS 23:32-35**
Jewish leaders approach Felix **ACTS 24:1-9**	*Paul before Felix* **ACTS 24:10-15**	*Paul before Felix* **ACTS 24:16-21**	*Paul in prison for two years* **ACTS 24:22-27**
Festus asks to see Paul **ACTS 25:1-8**	*Paul appeals to Caesar* **ACTS 25:9-12**	*Festus recounts to Agrippa* **ACTS 25:13-22**	*Paul brought before Agrippa* **ACTS 25:23-27**

Paul before Agrippa **ACTS 26:1-9**	*Paul before Agrippa* **ACTS 26:10-18**	*Paul before Agrippa* **ACTS 26:19-27**	*Agrippa almost persuaded* **ACTS 26:28-29**
Leaders discuss **ACTS 26:30-32**	*Paul and other prisoners put on ships* **ACTS 27:1-8**	*Voyage getting more dangerous* **ACTS 27:9-13**	*Ship is tossed with tempest* **ACTS 27:14-20**
Paul gives hope **ACTS 27:21-26**	*Shipmen listen to Paul* **ACTS 27:27-32**	*276 people on the ship* **ACTS 27:33-38**	*Ship wrecks on land* **ACTS 27:39-44**
People of island receive shipwrecked men **ACTS 28:1-2**	*Paul bit by viper* **ACTS 28:3-4**	*Paul thought to be a god* **ACTS 28:5-6**	*Paul heals sick* **ACTS 28:7-9**
Paul travels **ACTS 28:10-15**	*Paul preaches in Rome* **ACTS 28:16-20**	*Paul preaches in Rome* **ACTS 28:21-24**	*Paul preaches in Rome* **ACTS 28:25-31**

July 29 - August 4

Study these sections in *Come, Follow Me—For Individuals and Families: New Testament 2019*. As you study, record the teachings that stand out to you as well as any impressions you may receive. Be sure to make notes of any doctrines or principles you would like to discuss as a family in family home evening, family scripture study or in another setting.

1 *Disciples of Jesus Christ share their testimonies boldly.*

Acts 22:1–21; 26:1–29

2 *Why are there differences between the three accounts of Paul's vision of Jesus Christ?*

Acts 22:1–21; 26:9–20

3 *The Lord stands by those who strive to serve Him.*

Acts 23:10–11; 27:13–25, 40–44

4 *I can choose to accept or reject the words of God's servants.*

Acts 24:24–27; 26:1–3, 24–29; 27

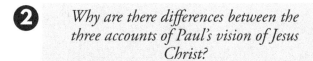

FAMILY HOME EVENING • FAMILY SCRIPTURE STUDY

MAKE A PLAN

In the space below, make a plan on WHAT and HOW you would like to teach your family. As you plan, prayerfully consider each member of the family with their learning levels and personal needs. Also, consider how different family members can contribute to the teaching of the rest of the family. They could make visual aids, study a particular topic and prepare to teach the family, research something, etc.

TEACHING IDEAS FOR YOU:

- To teach about Paul: Set the following items on a table with a sheet of paper next to each item. Write the scripture references noted at the top of the papers.

1. **A blindfold** (Paul was blinded) - Acts 22:1-16
2. **A paper that says "NO!"** (The people rejected Paul when he told him his conversion story) - Acts 22:22-23
3. **A picture of Christ** (The Lord appeared to Paul) - Acts 23:11
4. **A sword** (Jews plotted to kill Paul) - Acts 23:12-15
5. **A sheet/toga** (Felix was the governor from Rome set over Israel) - Acts 23:23-35
6. **Handcuffs / or something that represents prison** (Paul was in a Jerusalem prison for two years) - Acts 24:22-27
7. **A crown** (Agrippa was King Herod Agrippa, the Jewish king, and the last of the King Herods, or the Herodian dynasty) - Acts 25:23-27 and Acts 26:1-29
8. **A ship** (Paul was put on a ship and it was shipwrecked) - Acts 27:1-44
9. **A snake** (Paul was bitten by a snake) - Acts 28:1-6

- Together, learn about what each item means and how it represents something about Paul. As you go through each item, have the children draw or write what they learned about Paul (including any doctrines or principles). If someone says something insightful you could add it to the paper as well!
- Invite everyone to write or draw in their personal journals five things they learned about Paul.

ROMANS 1-6

The Power of God unto Salvation

AUGUST 5-11

As you study each set of verses, use the boxes to record what you are learning. Record the spiritual impressions you receive, the doctrinal truths you find, questions that come to mind, specific things you would like to teach your family, favorite phrases, etc. You can write, draw pictures, make diagrams... There is no right or wrong way.

Paul's salutation **ROMANS 1:1-15**	*I am not ashamed* **ROMANS 1:16-17**	*Those who change the truth about God* **ROMANS 1:18-25**	*When the truth of God is lost, this happens* **ROMANS 1:26-32**
Judgment of God **ROMANS 2:1-3**	*God leads to repentance* **ROMANS 2:4**	*Rewards for righteousness* **ROMANS 2:5-7**	*Punishment for sin* **ROMANS 2:8-9**
Hearers vs. doers **ROMANS 2:10-13**	*Instinctive righteousness* **ROMANS 2:14-16**	*Jews were hypocritical examples* **ROMANS 2:17-24**	*Inward vs. outward conversion* **ROMANS 2:25-29**
The Jews have the advantage of truth **ROMANS 3:1-2**	*Unbelief does not change truth* **ROMANS 3:3**	*God is justified in His judgments* **ROMANS 3:4-9**	*All men sin* **ROMANS 3:10-20**
Salvation comes through Christ **ROMANS 3:21-22**	*Mercy through the Atonement* **ROMANS 3:23-27**	*Honor the law of Moses by turning to Christ* **ROMANS 3:28-31**	*Abraham relied on Christ* **ROMANS 4:1-5**

Paul quotes David **ROMANS 4:6-8**	*Abraham was blessed before he was circumcised* **ROMANS 4:9-15**	*Faith, works, and grace* **ROMANS 4:16**	*Abraham's faith was tested* **ROMANS 4:17-22**
Abraham is our pattern **ROMANS 4:23-24**	*The Atonement of Jesus Christ* **ROMANS 4:25**	*Righteousness brings peace* **ROMANS 5:1-2**	*Blessing of hardship* **ROMANS 5:3**
Experience brings hope **ROMANS 5:4-5**	*Because God loves us, He sent His Son* **ROMANS 5:6-11**	*Adam brought death into the world* **ROMANS 5:12-15**	*Gift of Atonement comes through Christ* **ROMANS 5:16-17**
Adam brought death, Christ brought life **ROMANS 5:18-19**	*Christ overcame death* **ROMANS 5:20-21**	*Becoming dead to sin* **ROMANS 6:1-2**	*Symbol of baptism is death of sin* **ROMANS 6:3-5**
We become alive in Christ **ROMANS 6:6-11**	*Reject sin* **ROMANS 6:12-16**	*Servants of sin vs. Servants of righteousness* **ROMANS 6:17-20**	*Fruits of sin vs. Fruits of righteousness* **ROMANS 6:21-23**

Study these sections in *Come, Follow Me—For Individuals and Families: New Testament 2019.* As you study, record the teachings that stand out to you as well as any impressions you may receive. Be sure to make notes of any doctrines or principles you would like to discuss as a family in family home evening, family scripture study or in another setting.

1 *What are the epistles and how are they organized?*

Romans–Philemon

2 *When I show faith in the Savior by keeping His commandments, I am justified through His grace.*

Romans 1–6

3 *My outward actions must reflect and increase inner conversion.*

Romans 2:17–29

4 *Through Jesus Christ, I can be forgiven of my sins.*

Romans 3:10–31; 5

5 *The gospel of Jesus Christ invites me to "walk in newness of life."*

Romans 6

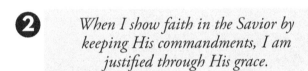

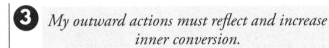

FAMILY HOME EVENING • FAMILY SCRIPTURE STUDY

MAKE A PLAN

In the space below, make a plan on WHAT and HOW you would like to teach your family. As you plan, prayerfully consider each member of the family with their learning levels and personal needs. Also, consider how different family members can contribute to the teaching of the rest of the family. They could make visual aids, study a particular topic and prepare to teach the family, research something, etc.

TEACHING IDEAS FOR YOU:

- To teach what an epistle is, before this lesson, write a letter to each of your children with your testimony and some important doctrines and principles. "Deliver" your letter to them and let them read it (you could also ask extended family to do the same and actually mail the letters). Explain that these are epistles, or letters. You wrote the epistles to help teach and strengthen someone you care about, just like the epistles in the Bible. Flip through the Bible and let the children see some of the epistles and how they begin (with a greeting). Explain that Paul wrote 14 out of the 21 epistles in the Bible. Paul's epistles are placed just after the Book of Acts and are arranged shortest to longest. The only exception is Hebrews. There was some disagreement among Bible scholars about whether Paul wrote Hebrews (some scholars believed that Luke wrote it) so it is placed behind Paul's shortest epistle. However, Joseph Smith attributed Hebrews as being from Paul. You could invite your children to write their own epistles to each other.

- Symbol of baptism. Have everyone draw the following picture in their journals:

Have everyone label their drawings as they read Romans 6: 1-11. Here are some tips for some context:

> *Paul reminded members of the Church that they had been "baptized into Jesus Christ," thus entering into a covenant relationship with Christ (see Romans 6:1–4). For Church members to choose to continue in sin was incompatible with that covenant relationship. Further, Paul taught that baptism symbolized being "buried with [Christ]" and becoming "dead … unto sin, but alive unto God" (Romans 6:4, 11). Baptism is a rebirth, symbolized by coming up out of the waters of baptism. Just as we were born into the world and became a living soul, so we must be born again and become a member of God's kingdom—both births involve the common elements of water, blood, and spirit (see Moses 6:59–60).*
> *- New Testament Seminary Student Manual (2018)*

> *"According to the Apostle Paul, baptism … denotes our descent into a watery grave from which we are raised with 'newness of life' (Romans 6:4) in Christ. The ordinance of baptism symbolizes Christ's death and Resurrection—we die with Him so we can live with Him" (Elder L. Tom Perry, "The Gospel of Jesus Christ," Ensign, May 2008, 46).*

Next to the "after baptism" drawing, invite everyone to write "walk in a newness of life" (from Romans 6:4). Have family members who have been baptized share how they have walked in a newness of life since their baptism and confirmation.

ROMANS 7–16

Overcome Evil with Good

AUGUST 12-18

As you study each set of verses, use the boxes to record what you are learning. Record the spiritual impressions you receive, the doctrinal truths you find, questions that come to mind, specific things you would like to teach your family, favorite phrases, etc. You can write, draw pictures, make diagrams... There is no right or wrong way.

Law of Moses is fulfilled **ROMANS 7:1-6**	*Paul benefited from the Law of Moses* **ROMANS 7:7-8**	*The Gospel replaced the Law of Moses* **ROMANS 7:9-13**	*The Gospel law helped Paul to become spiritual* **ROMANS 7:14-17**
Paul seeks to subdue the sin that dwells in him **ROMANS 7:18-25**	*Law of Christ replaced Law of Moses* **ROMANS 8:1-4**	*Law of Moses = Carnal* *Law of Christ = Spiritual* **ROMANS 8:5-6**	*Carnally vs. spiritually minded* **ROMANS 8:7-11**
Christians are debtors to Christ (not the Law of Moses) **ROMANS 8:12-13**	*Sons of God = Joint-heirs with Christ* **ROMANS 8:14-17**	*The glory that awaits us* **ROMANS 8:18-19**	*All men need to be saved by hope* **ROMANS 8:20-25**
The Spirit intervenes on our behalf **ROMANS 8:26-27**	*All things work for our good* **ROMANS 8:28**	*The called and elected* **ROMANS 8:29-31**	*God will give us all things* **ROMANS 8:32-34**
Those who are persecuted are more than conquerors **ROMANS 8:35-39**	*What God gave the House of Israel* **ROMANS 9:1-8**	*God chose Jacob over Esau* **ROMANS 9:9-13**	*God chose Israel to show His power through them* **ROMANS 9:14-23**

Jews and Gentiles will be saved **ROMANS 9:24-33**	*You have the word of God* **ROMANS 10:1-10**	*All who come unto Christ will be saved* **ROMANS 10:11-18**	*The Gentiles found the Lord* **ROMANS 10:19-21**
Not all Israel rejected Christ **ROMANS 11:1-6**	*Israel will sleep spiritually* **ROMANS 11:7-10**	*Israel will return* **ROMANS 11:11-15**	*Olive tree: Gentiles grafted into Israel* **ROMANS 11:16-24**
The fulness of the Gentiles **ROMANS 11:25-36**	*Present yourself as a living sacrifice* **ROMANS 12:1-3**	*Use your gifts* **ROMANS 12:4-8**	*How saints should live* **ROMANS 12:9-21**
Be subject to God's ministers **ROMANS 13:1-7**	*Put on armour of light* **ROMANS 13:8-14**	*Refrain from judging other church members* **ROMANS 14:1-13**	*Be mindful of the weak in faith* **ROMANS 14:14-23**
True saints fellowship each other **ROMANS 15:1-7**	*Gentiles were supposed to receive the Gospel* **ROMANS 15:8-13**	*Gentiles have been given gifts* **ROMANS 15:14-33**	*Messages to specific people in Rome* **ROMANS 16:1-27**

Study these sections in *Come, Follow Me—For Individuals and Families: New Testament 2019*. As you study, record the teachings that stand out to you as well as any impressions you may receive. Be sure to make notes of any doctrines or principles you would like to discuss as a family in family home evening, family scripture study or in another setting.

1 *If I follow the Spirit, I can overcome sin and prepare for an inheritance with God.*

Romans 7–8

2 *The eternal glory that awaits the faithful far outweighs the trials of mortality.*

Romans 8:17–39

3 *What did Paul mean by "predestinate," "election," and "foreknow"?*

Romans 8:29–30; 9–11

4 *Paul invites me to become a true Saint and follower of Jesus Christ.*

Romans 12–16

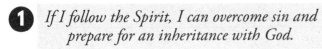

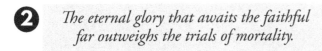

FAMILY HOME EVENING • FAMILY SCRIPTURE STUDY

MAKE A PLAN

In the space below, make a plan on WHAT and HOW you would like to teach your family. As you plan, prayerfully consider each member of the family with their learning levels and personal needs. Also, consider how different family members can contribute to the teaching of the rest of the family. They could make visual aids, study a particular topic and prepare to teach the family, research something, etc.

TEACHING IDEAS FOR YOU:

- Get a poster board and in the middle write "To the Romans". Pick out scriptures that you think would benefit your family to study and discuss. Write those references around the poster (suggestions below). Invite your family to study each scripture and write or draw the message they learned next to each reference. Some good scriptures to consider are:

    - Romans 8:16-18
    - Romans 8:28
    - Romans 9:31-32
    - Romans 10:17
    - Romans 12:1
    - Romans 14:10, 13

1 CORINTHIANS 1–7

"Be Perfectly Joined Together"

AUGUST 19-25

As you study each set of verses, use the boxes to record what you are learning. Record the spiritual impressions you receive, the doctrinal truths you find, questions that come to mind, specific things you would like to teach your family, favorite phrases, etc. You can write, draw pictures, make diagrams... There is no right or wrong way.

Paul's greeting to saints in Corinth **1 CORINTHIANS 1:1-9**	*Be unified* **1 CORINTHIANS 1:10-13**	*Preach to save souls* **1 CORINTHIANS 1:14-17**	*Truth only known by revelation, otherwise it seems foolish* **1 CORINTHIANS 1:18-25**
The Gospel is preached by the weak and simple **1 CORINTHIANS 1:26-31**	*Why we should teach by the Spirit* **1 CORINTHIANS 2:1-8**	*The Spirit reveals all things* **1 CORINTHIANS 2:9-16**	*Saints need to learn line upon line* **1 CORINTHIANS 3:1-2**
All are needed in the Church **1 CORINTHIANS 3:3-8**	*We are laborers together* **1 CORINTHIANS 3:9**	*Building the saints* **1 CORINTHIANS 3:10-15**	*Ye are the temple of God* **1 CORINTHIANS 3:16-17**
If faithful, we will inherit all things **1 CORINTHIANS 3:18-23**	*All ministers of Christ must be worthy* **1 CORINTHIANS 4:1-8**	*Apostles are persecuted* **1 CORINTHIANS 4:9-13**	*Follow Paul's example* **1 CORINTHIANS 4:14-17**

Paul is coming and will see if they teach with power **1 CORINTHIANS 4:18-21**	*A forbidden marriage* **1 CORINTHIANS 5:1-2**	*Such actions can hurt the Church* **1 CORINTHIANS 5:3-8**	*Sexually immoral cannot have Church membership* **1 CORINTHIANS 5:9-13**
Saints should avoid taking each other to court **1 CORINTHIANS 6:1-8**	*The unrighteous shall not be saved* **1 CORINTHIANS 6:9-14**	*The unrighteous shall not be saved* **1 CORINTHIANS 6:15-20**	*Marriage is honorable* **1 CORINTHIANS 7:1-5**
Paul's opinion on specific marital situations **1 CORINTHIANS 7:6-11**	*Counsel to spouses with mixed religious beliefs* **1 CORINTHIANS 7:12-14**	*Counsel to spouses with mixed religious beliefs* **1 CORINTHIANS 7:15-19**	*Counsel to members who are legal slaves* **1 CORINTHIANS 7:20-24**
Marriage status of missionaries in Paul's day **1 CORINTHIANS 7:25-28**	*Marriage status of missionaries in Paul's day* **1 CORINTHIANS 7:29-32**	*Marriage status of missionaries in Paul's day* **1 CORINTHIANS 7:33-36**	*Marriage status of missionaries in Paul's day* **1 CORINTHIANS 7:37-40**

August 19-25

Study these sections in *Come, Follow Me—For Individuals and Families: New Testament 2019*. As you study, record the teachings that stand out to you as well as any impressions you may receive. Be sure to make notes of any doctrines or principles you would like to discuss as a family in family home evening, family scripture study or in another setting.

1 *The members of Christ's Church are united.*

1 Corinthians 1:10–17; 3:1–11

2 *To accomplish God's work, I need the wisdom of God.*

1 Corinthians 1:17–31; 2

3 *I need the Holy Ghost in order to understand the things of God.*

1 Corinthians 2:9–16

4 *My body is sacred.*

1 Corinthians 6:13–20

5 *Did Paul teach that it is better to be unmarried than married?*

1 Corinthians 7:29–33

FAMILY HOME EVENING • FAMILY SCRIPTURE STUDY

MAKE A PLAN

In the space below, make a plan on WHAT and HOW you would like to teach your family. As you plan, prayerfully consider each member of the family with their learning levels and personal needs. Also, consider how different family members can contribute to the teaching of the rest of the family. They could make visual aids, study a particular topic and prepare to teach the family, research something, etc.

TEACHING IDEAS FOR YOU:

- Set up a road down the middle of your table. You could do this by having your children set up a toy road you might have, drawing a road on pieces of paper and taping them to each other down the table, or using "road car tape." Have them also draw or add some dangerous territories that might be along the side of the road (cliffs, ponds, etc.). Share this quote from Elder Joseph B. Wirthlin:

> *"While traveling along a mountainous road one evening through a driving rainstorm punctuated with frequent claps of thunder and flashes of lightning, Sister Wirthlin and I could barely see the road, either in front of us or to the right and the left. I watched the white lines on that road more intently than ever before. Staying within the lines kept us from going onto the shoulder and into the deep canyon on the one side and helped us avoid a head-on collision on the other. To wander over either line could have been very dangerous. Then I thought, 'Would a right-thinking person deviate to the left or the right of a traffic lane if he knew the result would be fatal? If he valued his mortal life, certainly he would stay between these lines.'*
>
> *"That experience traveling on this mountain road is so like life. If we stay within the lines that God has marked, he will protect us, and we can arrive safely at our destination" (in Conference Report, Oct. 1990, 80; or Ensign, Nov. 1990, 64).*

Explain that some of the saints in Corinth had begun to stray outside the teachings of the gospel (take a car down the road on your table and show it starting to swerve and get into dangerous territory). Ask: "What will happen if this car doesn't stay in the lines?" Paul wanted to help the saints before they strayed too far, so he wrote them this letter to teach correct doctrines and principles.

As you discuss the teachings in 1 Corinthians 1-7, have your children draw true teachings onto sticky notes and stick them down the center. They could also draw false teachings and stick them in the dangerous territory.

Use your scripture boxes on pages 130 and 131 in this book to determine what teachings would be best for you to teach the family. Some ideas are:

Scripture	*Topic*	*Things to draw on the "inside the lines"*	*Things to draw in dangerous territory*
1 Corinthians 1:10-13	Saints (and families) should be unified	Things your family can do to increase your unification	Things that would cause division in your family
1 Corinthians 6:18-20	Your body is a temple	Things you can do to honor your body and keep it a place the Spirit can dwell	Things that would defile your body
1 Corinthians 3:9-23	We must learn and teach by the Spirit (the natural man will think it is foolishness)	What we can do to learn by the Spirit What we can do to teach or preach by the Spirit	What will cause us not to learn by the Spirit What will cause us not to teach or preach by the Spirit

Have everyone write about what they learned in their personal journals. They could even draw their own road and write the teachings on it.

1 CORINTHIANS 8–13

Ye Are the Body of Christ

AUGUST 26 - SEPTEBMER 1

As you study each set of verses, use the boxes to record what you are learning. Record the spiritual impressions you receive, the doctrinal truths you find, questions that come to mind, specific things you would like to teach your family, favorite phrases, etc. You can write, draw pictures, make diagrams... There is no right or wrong way.

God knows his faithful followers **1 CORINTHIANS 8:1-3**	*Is it ok for members to eat meat meant for idols?* **1 CORINTHIANS 8:4**	*There are many gods in Heaven* **1 CORINTHIANS 8:5**
We worship Heavenly Father **1 CORINTHIANS 8:6**	*Be careful what others see you do* **1 CORINTHIANS 8:7-10**	*Do not eat if it offends a weaker saint* **1 CORINTHIANS 8:11-13**
Paul is an apostle **1 CORINTHIANS 9:1-2**	*Apostles have the right to marry* **1 CORINTHIANS 9:3-5**	*Leaders need support from members* **1 CORINTHIANS 9:6-12**
Woe is unto me if I preach not the gospel **1 CORINTHIANS 9:13-18**	*Paul is a servant to all* **1 CORINTHIANS 9:19-27**	*Christ is the God of Israel* **1 CORINTHIANS 10:1-4**

Ancient Israel rebelled against Christ **1 CORINTHIANS 10:5-15**	*True and False sacraments* **1 CORINTHIANS 10:16-33**	*Local customs for hair and grooming* **1 CORINTHIANS 11:1-15**
Heresies will arise **1 CORINTHIANS 11:16-19**	*Members acting inappropriately at Church* **1 CORINTHIANS 11:20-22**	*Why we should partake of the Sacrament* **1 CORINTHIANS 11:23-34**
The Holy Ghost reveals Jesus is the Christ **1 CORINTHIANS 12:1-3**	*Gifts of the Spirit* **1 CORINTHIANS 12:4-11**	*Every member has one or more gifts* **1 CORINTHIANS 12:12-31**
Why we need charity **1 CORINTHIANS 13:1-3**	*What charity is and is not* **1 CORINTHIANS 13:4-7**	*Charity never faileth* **1 CORINTHIANS 13:8-13**

Study these sections in *Come, Follow Me—For Individuals and Families: New Testament 2019*. As you study, record the teachings that stand out to you as well as any impressions you may receive. Be sure to make notes of any doctrines or principles you would like to discuss as a family in family home evening, family scripture study or in another setting.

1 *God provides a way to escape temptation.*

1 Corinthians 10:1–13

2 *The sacrament unifies us as followers of Christ.*

1 Corinthians 10:16–17; 11:16–30

3 *Why did Paul write about head coverings and hairstyles?*

1 Corinthians 11:3–15

4 *Spiritual gifts are given to benefit all of Heavenly Father's children.*

1 Corinthians 12–13

FAMILY HOME EVENING • FAMILY SCRIPTURE STUDY

MAKE A PLAN

In the space below, make a plan on WHAT and HOW you would like to teach your family. As you plan, prayerfully consider each member of the family with their learning levels and personal needs. Also, consider how different family members can contribute to the teaching of the rest of the family. They could make visual aids, study a particular topic and prepare to teach the family, research something, etc.

TEACHING IDEAS FOR YOU:

- Before the lesson, think of a spiritual gift that each member of your family has. Write the gifts on separate pieces of paper and put each one in a box and wrap them. Set them on the table with each person's name on their box. Together, open to 1 Corinthians 12:4-11 and explain that Paul wanted to teach the saints about spiritual gifts, which many saints did not understand correctly. Make a list of all of the gifts of the Spirit described in those verses. Paul taught that there are many spiritual gifts that work in different ways but that all come from God through the Holy Ghost. Gifts of the Spirit are blessings or abilities given through the Holy Ghost and God gives at least one gift to every member of the Church.

In your journals or on a poster board, make a list of the gifts of the Spirit that Paul mentions in verses 8-11. Next to each gift, write what you think that gift means and times you have seen that gift in someone.

Share and discuss these quotes (and have everyone write what they learn in their personal journals).

→ *"Taken at random, let me mention a few gifts that are not always evident or noteworthy but that are very important. …*
"Let us review some of these less-conspicuous gifts: the gift of asking; the gift of listening; the gift of hearing and using a still, small voice; the gift of being able to weep; the gift of avoiding contention; the gift of being agreeable; the gift of avoiding vain repetition; the gift of seeking that which is righteous; the gift of not passing judgment; the gift of looking to God for guidance; the gift of being a disciple; the gift of caring for others; the gift of being able to ponder; the gift of offering prayer; the gift of bearing a mighty testimony; and the gift of receiving the Holy Ghost" ("Elder Marvin J. Ashton, There Are Many Gifts,*" Ensign,* Nov. 1987, 20*)*.

→ *"Spiritual gifts are endless in number and infinite in variety" (*Elder Bruce R. McConkie, *A New Witness for the Articles of Faith* [1985], 371*)*.

→ *"Following our baptism, each of us had those holding the Melchizedek Priesthood lay hands on our heads for us to receive the gift of the Holy Ghost. If we are faithful, we can have His influence with us. Through Him, we each can be blessed with certain spiritual powers called gifts of the Spirit. These gifts are given to those who are faithful to Christ. They will help us know and teach the truths of the gospel. They will help us bless others. They will guide us back to our Heavenly Father (*Elder Robert D. Hales, *Ensign,* February 2002*)*.

→ *"If any of us are imperfect, it is our duty to pray for the gift that will make us perfect. … No man ought to say, 'Oh, I cannot help this; it is my nature.' He is not justified in it, for the reason that God has promised to give strength to correct these things, and to give gifts that will eradicate them. If a man lack wisdom, it is his duty to ask God for wisdom. The same with everything else. That is the design of God concerning His Church. He wants His Saints to be perfected in the truth. For this purpose He gives these gifts, and bestows them upon those who seek after them, in order that they may be a perfect people upon the face of the earth" (*President George Q. Cannon, *Millennial Star,* 23 Apr. 1894, 260*)*.

Explain that you have recognized spiritual gifts in each person in the family, and that gift is on the table, wrapped up. Have everyone take their gift and before they open it invite everyone to guess what might be in each person's box (this will invite sharing of what gifts they recognize in one another. Let them open their gifts and talk about what you wrote.

Invite everyone to consider what gifts they would like to have and make a list in their personal journals.

1 CORINTHIANS 14–16

God Is Not the Author of Confusion, but of Peace

SEPTEMBER 2-8

As you study each set of verses, use the boxes to record what you are learning. Record the spiritual impressions you receive, the doctrinal truths you find, questions that come to mind, specific things you would like to teach your family, favorite phrases, etc. You can write, draw pictures, make diagrams... There is no right or wrong way.

Desire spiritual gifts **1 CORINTHIANS 14:1**	*Gift of tongues vs. gift of prophecy* **1 CORINTHIANS 14:2-9**	*Gift of tongues vs. gift of prophecy* **1 CORINTHIANS 14:10-19**
Gift of tongues vs. gift of prophecy **1 CORINTHIANS 14:20-28**	*Ye may all prophesy* **1 CORINTHIANS 14:29-31**	*Order in Church* **1 CORINTHIANS 14:32-38**
Covet to prophesy **1 CORINTHIANS 14:39-40**	*Christ died for our sins* **1 CORINTHIANS 15:1-11**	*Christ was resurrected* **1 CORINTHIANS 15:12-20**

All will be resurrected
1 CORINTHIANS 15:21-22

Order of resurrection
1 CORINTHIANS 15:23-28

Baptism for the dead
1 CORINTHIANS 15:29

A better resurrection
1 CORINTHIANS 15:30-34

Kingdoms of glory
1 CORINTHIANS 15:35-42

Victory over death comes through Christ
1 CORINTHIANS 15:43-58

Paul's parting words
1 CORINTHIANS 16:1-8

Paul's parting words
1 CORINTHIANS 16:9-16

Pauls' parting words
1 CORINTHIANS 16:17-24

Study these sections in *Come, Follow Me—For Individuals and Families: New Testament 2019.* As you study, record the teachings that stand out to you as well as any impressions you may receive. Be sure to make notes of any doctrines or principles you would like to discuss as a family in family home evening, family scripture study or in another setting.

1 *I can seek the gift of prophecy.*

1 Corinthians 14

2 *Why did Paul say women should keep silent in church?*

1 Corinthians 14:34–35

3 *Jesus Christ gained victory over death.*

1 Corinthians 15:1–34, 53–58

4 *Resurrected bodies are different from mortal bodies.*

1 Corinthians 15:35–54

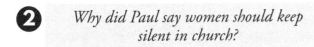

FAMILY HOME EVENING • FAMILY SCRIPTURE STUDY

MAKE A PLAN

In the space below, make a plan on WHAT and HOW you would like to teach your family. As you plan, prayerfully consider each member of the family with their learning levels and personal needs. Also, consider how different family members can contribute to the teaching of the rest of the family. They could make visual aids, study a particular topic and prepare to teach the family, research something, etc.

TEACHING IDEAS FOR YOU:

- Lay out several comforting items such as blankets, certain stuffed animals your children love, and lit candles. Light a fire in the fireplace, have a "comfort meal" for dinner, have soft music playing, etc. Ask everyone how they feel and explain that you have tried to surround everyone with items that bring comfort. Identify what each item is and talk about why they are things that bring comfort.

Explain that one reason people are drawn to the gospel is because there are many comforting doctrines that answer life's most vexing questions. Ask everyone to ponder and share what those vexing questions might be.

In the center of the table have a stack of papers with a situation written on each paper with scripture references underneath (see below for examples). Go through each question with your family and discuss what Paul taught about the answer to that question. When you are done, have everyone write or draw what they learned in their journals.

1. My grandpa died and he was never a member of the Church. (1 Corinthians 15:29)
2. My friend died and I don't know where he is or if I will ever see him again. (1 Corinthians 15:34-35)
* See also "Resurrection" and "Kingdoms of Glory" in *True to the Faith.*
3. Why should I try so hard to be good? (1 Corinthians 15:40-41) See also "Kingdoms of Glory" in *True to the Faith.*

You can also share the story by President Thomas S. Monson in his talk, "Mrs. Patton—the Story Continues," *Ensign*, Nov. 2007, 21–24; see also the video "Until We Meet Again (found on the Church's website)."

2 CORINTHIANS 1-7

Be Ye Reconciled to God

SEPTEMBER 9-15

As you study each set of verses, use the boxes to record what you are learning. Record the spiritual impressions you receive, the doctrinal truths you find, questions that come to mind, specific things you would like to teach your family, favorite phrases, etc. You can write, draw pictures, make diagrams... There is no right or wrong way.

Greeting **2 CORINTHIANS 1:1-3**	*Those who suffer* **2 CORINTHIANS 1:4-7**	*Pray for Paul and Timothy* **2 CORINTHIANS 1:8-14**
The saints are promised blessings **2 CORINTHIANS 1:15-19**	*The saints are promised blessings* **2 CORINTHIANS 1:20-24**	*Saints should love and forgive one another* **2 CORINTHIANS 2:1-5**
Saints should love and forgive one another **2 CORINTHIANS 2:6-11**	*Saints triumph in Christ* **2 CORINTHIANS 2:12-17**	*The scriptures are written upon us* **2 CORINTHIANS 3:1-4**
Ministers of the new testament **2 CORINTHIANS 3:5-11**	*The vail is done away* **2 CORINTHIANS 3:12-18**	*Shine the gospel for those that are lost* **2 CORINTHIANS 4:1-7**

Mortal trials vs. Eternal glory **2 CORINTHIANS 4:8-13**	*Mortal trials vs. Eternal glory* **2 CORINTHIANS 4:14-18**	*Saints seek immortality* **2 CORINTHIANS 5:1-4**
We must all appear at Judgment Seat **2 CORINTHIANS 5:5-11**	*The Gospel reconciles man to God* **2 CORINTHIANS 5:12-19**	*Ambassadors for Christ* **2 CORINTHIANS 5:20-21**
Now is the day of salvation **2 CORINTHIANS 6:1-2**	*God's ministers must be righteous* **2 CORINTHIANS 6:3-10**	*Do not be unequally yoked with unbelievers* **2 CORINTHIANS 6:11-18**
Let us repent **2 CORINTHIANS 7:1-8**	*Godly sorrow worketh repentance* **2 CORINTHIANS 7:9-11**	*Paul boasts of saints* **2 CORINTHIANS 7:12-16**

Study these sections in *Come, Follow Me—For Individuals and Families: New Testament 2019.* As you study, record the teachings that stand out to you as well as any impressions you may receive. Be sure to make notes of any doctrines or principles you would like to discuss as a family in family home evening, family scripture study or in another setting.

1 *My trials can be a blessing.*

2 Corinthians 1:3–7; 4:6–10, 17–18; 7:4–7

2 *I receive blessings and bless others when I forgive.*

2 Corinthians 2:5–11

3 *Through the Atonement of Jesus Christ, I can be reconciled to God.*

2 Corinthians 5:14–21

4 *Godly sorrow leads to repentance.*

2 Corinthians 7:8–11

FAMILY HOME EVENING • FAMILY SCRIPTURE STUDY

MAKE A PLAN

In the space below, make a plan on WHAT and HOW you would like to teach your family. As you plan, prayerfully consider each member of the family with their learning levels and personal needs. Also, consider how different family members can contribute to the teaching of the rest of the family. They could make visual aids, study a particular topic and prepare to teach the family, research something, etc.

TEACHING IDEAS FOR YOU:

- To teach your children about walking by faith and not by sight, blindfold each of them and take the whole family on a faith walk. You do this by blindfolding them and leading them around the house and yard either by hand, or by giving them verbal instructions. Pay attention to parts that are hard for them, or when their faith waivered (possibly when the stakes are higher, like on the stairs).

When they are finished ask them questions such as:

- What was that experience like for you?
- What was the hardest part?
- What was the easiest part?
- Why did you listen to my instructions?

Turn to 2 Corinthians 5:6-7 and read and discuss those scriptures. See if everyone can memorize verse 7. You might want to take this opportunity to make sure they understand the doctrine of the Premortal life and that we experienced having a veil of forgetfulness being drawn over our minds.

Share about some times in your life that you have walked by faith instead of by sight and experienced great blessings for it. Ask the children to share times they have also had that experience.

In everyone's journals, have them write the scripture in 2 Corinthians 5:7 and make a list of times in their lives they will yet experience when they might need to walk by faith.

2 CORINTHIANS 8-13

God Loveth a Cheerful Giver

SEPTEMBER 16–22

As you study each set of verses, use the boxes to record what you are learning. Record the spiritual impressions you receive, the doctrinal truths you find, questions that come to mind, specific things you would like to teach your family, favorite phrases, etc. You can write, draw pictures, make diagrams... There is no right or wrong way.

Members liberally gave **2 CORINTHIANS 8:1-8**	*Christ left Heaven to be mortal and bring eternal riches* **2 CORINTHIANS 8:9**	*Donations based on ability to pay* **2 CORINTHIANS 8:10-15**
The missionary Titus **2 CORINTHIANS 8:16-24**	*The saints are willing givers* **2 CORINTHIANS 9:1-3**	*God loves the cheerful giver* **2 CORINTHIANS 9:4-7**
Blessings flow to those who give **2 CORINTHIANS 9:8-11**	*Your generosity can bring others to God* **2 CORINTHIANS 9:12-15**	*God helps us overcome the world* **2 CORINTHIANS 10:1-6**
Paul glories in the Lord **2 CORINTHIANS 10:7-18**	*Paul is protective of saints* **2 CORINTHIANS 11:1-3**	*Paul has tried to teach them* **2 CORINTHIANS 11:4-11**

False prophets and ministers **2 CORINTHIANS 11:12-15**	*Paul's experiences* **2 CORINTHIANS 11:16-21**	*Paul's experiences* **2 CORINTHIANS 11:22-33**
Paul caught up into third heaven **2 CORINTHIANS 12:1-3**	*Paul caught up into third heaven* **2 CORINTHIANS 12:4-6**	*Paul glories in his weaknesses* **2 CORINTHIANS 12:7-10**
Signs of an apostle **2 CORINTHIANS 12:11-15**	*Signs of an apostle* **2 CORINTHIANS 12:16-21**	*Witnesses* **2 CORINTHIANS 13:1-4**
Examine yourselves **2 CORINTHIANS 13:5-7**	*Examine yourselves* **2 CORINTHIANS 13:8-10**	*Farewell* **2 CORINTHIANS 13:11-14**

2 Corinthians 8–13

September 16–22

Study these sections in *Come, Follow Me—For Individuals and Families: New Testament 2019*. As you study, record the teachings that stand out to you as well as any impressions you may receive. Be sure to make notes of any doctrines or principles you would like to discuss as a family in family home evening, family scripture study or in another setting.

1 *I can cheerfully share what I have to bless the poor and needy.*

2 Corinthians 8:1–15; 9:5–15

2 *False prophets seek to deceive.*

2 Corinthians 11

3 *I should "examine" my faithfulness in the gospel of Jesus Christ.*

2 Corinthians 11:3; 13:5–8

4 *What is "the third heaven," and who was the man who was "caught up to" it?*

2 Corinthians 12:2–4

5 *The Savior's grace is sufficient to help me find strength in my weakness.*

2 Corinthians 12:5–10

6 *What did Paul mean when he spoke of "two or three witnesses"?*

2 Corinthians 13:1

FAMILY HOME EVENING • FAMILY SCRIPTURE STUDY

MAKE A PLAN

In the space below, make a plan on WHAT and HOW you would like to teach your family. As you plan, prayerfully consider each member of the family with their learning levels and personal needs. Also, consider how different family members can contribute to the teaching of the rest of the family. They could make visual aids, study a particular topic and prepare to teach the family, research something, etc.

TEACHING IDEAS FOR YOU:

- 2 Corinthians 12:1-6 is a great place to teach about the Plan of Salvation, specifically the kingdoms of glory. Cut out three large circles out of poster board and lay them on the table. Using *True to the Faith* (found online or on your Gospel Library app), look up "Kingdoms of Glory." Have your family make a visual on each circle of the three kingdoms of glory. They can draw things within each circle that they learn about each kingdom (including the name, who will live there, details they learn about it, etc.). You can also find quotes, look up other scripture references, etc.

- To teach 2 Corinthians 9:6-7, have one of your family members draw a picture of two farmers on their farms. Have one farmer standing in his field that is full of what he planted (wheat, corn, etc.) because he planted many seeds. Have the other farmer standing in his field that has grown, but it is not full because he planted fewer seeds.

Invite your family to read 2 Corinthians 9:6-7, and, if possible, memorize it (and write it in their personal journals). Discuss the analogy of the farmers on the drawings compared to what we sow and reap in our lives, and discuss what a "cheerful giver" is. Make a list of people you know who are cheerful givers and have reaped many blessings from it. Invite everyone to pray and seek for inspiration on how your family can be of service to a family, group, or someone in need. Tell them to keep notes in their personal journals of any thoughts or ideas they have of who they can serve. Each night (during dinner or another time) review the scripture they memorized and ask if they have received any answers on who they can serve. * This is also a great time to help them learn to recognize when they receive revelation.

GALATIANS

Walk in the Spirit

SEPTEMBER 23–29

As you study each set of verses, use the boxes to record what you are learning. Record the spiritual impressions you receive, the doctrinal truths you find, questions that come to mind, specific things you would like to teach your family, favorite phrases, etc. You can write, draw pictures, make diagrams... There is no right or wrong way.

Greeting **GALATIANS 1:1-5**	*Members apostatizing* **GALATIANS 1:6-7**	*Preachers that teach a false gospel* **GALATIANS 1:8-10**	*True gospel not received by man - but by the Spirit* **GALATIANS 1:11-12**
God called Paul **GALATIANS 1:13-15**	*Paul went forth and preached* **GALATIANS 1: 16-24**	*Paul made sure the doctrine he taught was correct* **GALATIANS 2:1-2**	*Titus did not need circumcision* **GALATIANS 2:3-5**
Peter primarily taught Jews, and Paul taught Gentiles **GALATIANS 2:6-9**	*Jewish Christians were still living Mosaic Law and customs* **GALATIANS 2:10-14**	*Let go of the old law* **GALATIANS 2:15-19**	*Paul crucified the natural man in him* **GALATIANS 2:20-21**
Turn back to the gospel and away from the law of Moses **GALATIANS 3:1-6**	*Promises to family of Abraham* **GALATIANS 3:7-9**	*The Law of Moses cannot save you* **GALATIANS 3:10-15**	*Abraham's posterity* **GALATIANS 3:16-18**
The Law of Moses was given because Israelites were not able to receive Higher Law **GALATIANS 3:19-23**	*Law of Moses prepared Israelites for Higher Law* **GALATIANS 3:24-25**	*Gentiles also belong to Abraham* **GALATIANS 3:26-29**	*The Law of Moses tutored them* **GALATIANS 4:1-5**

Gentiles are sons and heirs **GALATIANS 4:6-7**	*You had accepted Christ - come back* **GALATIANS 4:8-13**	*You had accepted Christ - come back* **GALATIANS 4:14-20**	*An allegory: Comparing the gospel to the Law of Moses* **GALATIANS 4:21-26**
An allegory: Comparing the gospel to the Law of Moses **GALATIANS 4:27-31**	*Don't entangle in old beliefs* **GALATIANS 5:1-4**	*Seek faith, love, and the Spirit* **GALATIANS 5:5-9**	*Seek faith, love, and the Spirit* **GALATIANS 5:10-15**
The Spirit protects you from lust of sin **GALATIANS 5:16-18**	*The lusts of flesh* **GALATIANS 5:19-21**	*The fruits of the Spirit* **GALATIANS 5:22-23**	*How saints should be* **GALATIANS 5:24-26**
Bear one another's burdens **GALATIANS 6:1-3**	*Bear one another's burdens* **GALATIANS 6:4-6**	*What ye sow, ye shall reap* **GALATIANS 6:7-9**	*Do good* **GALATIANS 6:10**
Do not fear persecution **GALATIANS 6:11-12**	*Do not fear persecution* **GALATIANS 6:13-14**	*The gospel is for all* **GALATIANS 6:15-16**	*Paul's scars show he has faced persecution* **GALATIANS 6:17-18**

September 23–29

Study these sections in *Come, Follow Me—For Individuals and Families: New Testament 2019.* As you study, record the teachings that stand out to you as well as any impressions you may receive. Be sure to make notes of any doctrines or principles you would like to discuss as a family in family home evening, family scripture study or in another setting.

1 *The law of Christ makes me free.*

Galatians 1–5

2 *I am an heir to the blessings promised to Abraham.*

Galatians 3

3 *Did Abraham have the gospel of Jesus Christ?*

Galatians 3:6–25

4 *If I "walk in the Spirit," I will receive the "fruit of the Spirit."*

Galatians 5:13–26; 6:7–10

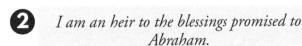

FAMILY HOME EVENING • FAMILY SCRIPTURE STUDY

MAKE A PLAN

In the space below, make a plan on WHAT and HOW you would like to teach your family. As you plan, prayerfully consider each member of the family with their learning levels and personal needs. Also, consider how different family members can contribute to the teaching of the rest of the family. They could make visual aids, study a particular topic and prepare to teach the family, research something, etc.

TEACHING IDEAS FOR YOU:

- To teach about the fruits of the Spirit, have your children make a large tree out of poster board. Cut out several small apples, pears, or other fruit that grows on a tree. Tell your children to imagine that you just moved into a home and there is a fruit tree in the yard, but you don't know what kind of a tree it is. Ask them when you will know for certain what kind of a tree it is (when the fruits appear on the tree).

Have your family turn to Galatians 5:22-23 and look for the kind of fruits Paul is talking about (the fruits of the Spirit). Have your children label the trunk on the tree they made, "the Holy Ghost," and label the fruits you cut out with the fruits Paul describes in verses 22 and 23, and then put them on the tree. Explain that when someone has the Holy Ghost or Spirit with them, these are the fruits or results they will experience.

Talk about each fruit and what it means, and what it looks like in your home when your family is experiencing that fruit. Make a list of things you can do to have the Spirit in your home so that those fruits are in your home continually.

You could also use the tree to talk about these questions:

- Why would you also want to experience these fruits of the Spirit when you are at school?
- What can you do to have the Spirit with you while you are at school?
- Why would you also want to experience these fruits of the Spirit when you are with your friends?
- What can you do to have the Spirit with you while you are with your friends?

Have everyone write (or draw) a list of the fruits of the Spirit in their personal journals and also make a list of things they will do to cultivate those gifts of the Spirit. You could also have your favorite fruit dish or dessert together.

* Fun idea: Do you have tablecloths, clothes, or dishes with fruits on them? Use them for dinner or during the lesson.

EPHESIANS

For the Perfecting of the Saints

SEPTEMBER 30–OCTOBER 13

As you study each set of verses, use the boxes to record what you are learning. Record the spiritual impressions you receive, the doctrinal truths you find, questions that come to mind, specific things you would like to teach your family, favorite phrases, etc. You can write, draw pictures, make diagrams... There is no right or wrong way.

Greeting **EPHESIANS 1:1-3**	*Saints have been foreordained* **EPHESIANS 1:4-8**	*Gospel to be restored in latter-days* **EPHESIANS 1:9-12**	*Holy Spirit of Promise* **EPHESIANS 1:13-14**
Holy Ghost reveals God and Jesus Christ **EPHESIANS 1:15-23**	*Formerly walked after Satan* **EPHESIANS 2:1-3**	*Because God loves us* **EPHESIANS 2:4-7**	*We are saved by grace through faith* **EPHESIANS 2:8-10**
Blood of Christ saves Jews and Gentiles **EPHESIANS 2:11-18**	*Gentiles are not strangers* **EPHESIANS 2:19**	*Church built upon foundation of prophets and apostles* **EPHESIANS 2:20-22**	*Jews and Gentiles are fellow heirs* **EPHESIANS 3:1-13**
Love Christ **EPHESIANS 3:14-21**	*One Lord & one baptism* **EPHESIANS 4:1-10**	*The Lord gave us apostles and prophets* **EPHESIANS 4:11-16**	*How Christ's followers should live* **EPHESIANS 4:17-24**

How Christ's followers should live **EPHESIANS 4:25-32**	*How followers of God should walk* **EPHESIANS 5:1-5**	*Be not deceived* **EPHESIANS 5:6-7**	*Walk as children of light* **EPHESIANS 5:8-10**
Works of darkness **EPHESIANS 5:11-13**	*Walk as the wise* **EPHESIANS 5:14-21**	*Husbands and wives should love each other* **EPHESIANS 5:22-33**	*Children should obey parents* **EPHESIANS 6:1-3**
Parents should teach **EPHESIANS 6:4**	*How to live under Ephesian slavery law* **EPHESIANS 6:5-9**	*Put on the whole armour of God* **EPHESIANS 6:10-13**	*The armour of God* **EPHESIANS 6:14**
The armour of God **EPHESIANS 6:15**	*The armour of God* **EPHESIANS 6:16**	*The armour of God* **EPHESIANS 6:17**	*Pray always / Paul's farewell* **EPHESIANS 6:18-24**

September 30–October 13

Study these sections in *Come, Follow Me—For Individuals and Families: New Testament 2019.* As you study, record the teachings that stand out to you as well as any impressions you may receive. Be sure to make notes of any doctrines or principles you would like to discuss as a family in family home evening, family scripture study or in another setting.

1 *Has God "chosen" or "predestinated" some of His children to be saved?*

Ephesians 1:4–11, 17–19

2 *God will "gather together in one all things in Christ."*

Ephesians 1:10

3 *The Church is founded on apostles and prophets, and Jesus Christ is the chief cornerstone.*

Ephesians 2:19–22; 4:11–16

4 *I can strengthen my family relationships.*

Ephesians 5:21–6:4

5 *Putting on "the whole armour of God" will help protect me from evil.*

Ephesians 6:10–18

FAMILY HOME EVENING • FAMILY SCRIPTURE STUDY

MAKE A PLAN

In the space below, make a plan on WHAT and HOW you would like to teach your family. As you plan, prayerfully consider each member of the family with their learning levels and personal needs. Also, consider how different family members can contribute to the teaching of the rest of the family. They could make visual aids, study a particular topic and prepare to teach the family, research something, etc.

TEACHING IDEAS FOR YOU:

Ask your children what they do to protect themselves from the rain. What do they do to protect themselves from getting hurt in a car accident? What do they do to protect themselves from getting sick? What do they do to protect themselves while riding their bike? And then finally, what do they do to protect themselves from Satan's evil influences?

Tell your children that Paul explained a very good way for us to protect ourselves from Satan. In their personal journals, have each person draw a picture of themselves. Once they are finished, they need to add certain pieces of armor to their picture. Together, read Ephesians 6:10-18 to discover what to add (you can find some "Armor of God" (also Armour) pictures easily online if they need some visual examples of what to draw.

Have them label what each piece of armor represents. You can use the descriptions below if they need help understanding. They come from *The Friend*, June 2016.

- **Helmet of Salvation:** A helmet protects the head. We keep our minds safe when we follow Jesus and do what He wants us to do.
- **Shield of Faith:** Faith in Jesus Christ protects us like a shield. When we believe in Jesus and try to be like Him, we can make good choices, even when things are hard.
- **Girdle of Truth:** A girdle is a belt that helps protect a soldier's body. Knowing what is true protects us. The gospel is true, and living the gospel makes us strong.
- **Breastplate of Righteousness:** The breastplate protects the heart. When we love God with all our heart, we try to keep His commandments. We are blessed when we choose the right.
- **Shoes of the Preparation of Peace:** Shoes protect the feet. We try to follow Jesus Christ's footsteps so we can live with Him someday.
- **Sword of the Spirit:** A sword helps fight against wrong. The Spirit helps us when we face bad or hard things. Listening to the Spirit helps us stay safe.

Once they have everything labeled, talk through each item and how they can make that part of their armor really strong. In their journals they could make lists of things they can do next to each part of the armor. For example, next to "Helmet" you might put to not watch inappropriate movies, tell bad jokes, etc.

You could even take each day of the week to focus on one part of the armor. So, on Tuesday you might focus on the helmet, on Wednesday the shield, etc.

PHILIPPIANS; COLOSSIANS

I Can Do All Things through Christ Which Strengtheneth Me

OCTOBER 14-20

As you study each set of verses, use the boxes to record what you are learning. Record the spiritual impressions you receive, the doctrinal truths you find, questions that come to mind, specific things you would like to teach your family, favorite phrases, etc. You can write, draw pictures, make diagrams... There is no right or wrong way.

Greeting **PHILIPPIANS 1:1-8**	*Seek love more and more* **PHILIPPIANS 1:9-11**	*All that happened to Paul furthered the gospel* **PHILIPPIANS 1:12-15**	*All that happened to Paul furthered the gospel* **PHILIPPIANS 1:16-19**
Paul does not fear death **PHILIPPIANS 1:20-23**	*Paul does not fear death* **PHILIPPIANS 1:24-26**	*The conduct of saints* **PHILIPPIANS 1:27-30**	*Saints should live in harmony* **PHILIPPIANS 2:1-4**
Christ has been exalted **PHILIPPIANS 2:5-9**	*Every knee shall bow* **PHILIPPIANS 2:10-11**	*Saints must work out own salvation* **PHILIPPIANS 2:12-16**	*Paul's outlook on martyrdom* **PHILIPPIANS 2:17-30**
Paul sacrifices all things in Christ **PHILIPPIANS 3:1-6**	*Paul sacrifices all things in Christ* **PHILIPPIANS 3:7-12**	*True ministers set examples of righteousness* **PHILIPPIANS 3:13-17**	*True ministers set examples of righteousness* **PHILIPPIANS 3:18-21**
Stand fast in the Lord **PHILIPPIANS 4:1-7**	*The gospel embraces all truth* **PHILIPPIANS 4:8-10**	*I can do all things* **PHILIPPIANS 4:11-13**	*Farewell* **PHILIPPIANS 4:14-23**

Greeting **COLOSSIANS 1:1-8**	*Paul's desires for Saints* **COLOSSIANS 1:9-12**	*What we have through Christ* **COLOSSIANS 1:13-15**	*What we have through Christ* **COLOSSIANS 1:16-20**
Be not moved **COLOSSIANS 1:21-24**	*Gospel preached to every man* **COLOSSIANS 1:25-29**	*Fulness of Godhead dwells in Christ* **COLOSSIANS 2:1-7**	*Beware of traditions of men* **COLOSSIANS 2:8**
What you get through Christ **COLOSSIANS 2:9-13**	*Christ blotted out the Law of Moses* **COLOSSIANS 2:14-15**	*Let no man do these things* **COLOSSIANS 2:16-18**	*Be dead with Christ* **COLOSSIANS 2:19-23**
Set your affections on things above **COLOSSIANS 3:1-4**	*Be holy* **COLOSSIANS 3:5-9**	*Be holy* **COLOSSIANS 3:10-17**	*Wise teachings* **COLOSSIANS 3:18-21**
Wise teachings **COLOSSIANS 3:22-25**	*Wise teachings* **COLOSSIANS 4:1-4**	*Wise teachings* **COLOSSIANS 4:5-8**	*Paul speaks to specific individuals* **COLOSSIANS 4:9-18**

October 14-20

Study these sections in *Come, Follow Me—For Individuals and Families: New Testament 2019.* As you study, record the teachings that stand out to you as well as any impressions you may receive. Be sure to make notes of any doctrines or principles you would like to discuss as a family in family home evening, family scripture study or in another setting.

1 *Do we "work out [our] own salvation"?*

Philippians 2:12–13

2 *The gospel of Jesus Christ is worth every sacrifice.*

Philippians 3:5–14

3 *I can find joy in Christ, regardless of my circumstances.*

Philippians 4:1–13

4 *My faith is founded on Jesus Christ.*

Colossians 1:12–23

5 *Disciples of Jesus Christ become "new" as they live His gospel.*

Colossians 3:1–17

FAMILY HOME EVENING • FAMILY SCRIPTURE STUDY

MAKE A PLAN

In the space below, make a plan on WHAT and HOW you would like to teach your family. As you plan, prayerfully consider each member of the family with their learning levels and personal needs. Also, consider how different family members can contribute to the teaching of the rest of the family. They could make visual aids, study a particular topic and prepare to teach the family, research something, etc.

TEACHING IDEAS FOR YOU:

- To teach Philippians 4:13 ("I can do all things through Christ which strenghtheneth me"), put out a jar in the middle of the table or room and label it "The Worry Jar." Have slips of paper out and have everyone write on at least 3 pieces of paper things they are currently worried about and have them put them in the jar.

Explain that we all worry about things, but Paul gave us a scripture that can help us with every worry in that jar. Invite everyone to read Philippians 4:13. See if everyone can memorize it so they can call upon it when needed. They can also write the entire scripture in their personal journals.

Share this quote by President Dieter F. Uchtdorf, and have everyone add the quote to their personal journals:

> *"God pours out blessings of power and strength, enabling us to achieve things that otherwise would be far beyond our reach. It is by God's amazing grace that His children can overcome the undercurrents and quicksands of the deceiver, rise above sin, and 'be perfect[ed] in Christ' [Moroni 10:32]" ("The Gift of Grace," Ensign or Liahona, May 2015, 108).*

Share one or two times that you were worried about something, but turned to Christ and He strengthened you. Invite others to also share.

Go back to The Worry Jar and pull out a slip. Read it out loud and ask everyone to guess who wrote it. As a family, discuss how turning to Christ might help them in that situation and what some specific things are that they could pray for that would strengthen them. Continue until you have gone through all of the slips.

Challenge your family to apply this scripture to their lives throughout the week and to pray for each other's concerns in their daily prayers.

1 AND 2 THESSALONIANS

Be Not Soon Shaken in Mind, or Be Troubled

OCTOBER 21–27

As you study each set of verses, use the boxes to record what you are learning. Record the spiritual impressions you receive, the doctrinal truths you find, questions that come to mind, specific things you would like to teach your family, favorite phrases, etc. You can write, draw pictures, make diagrams... There is no right or wrong way.

Greeting **1 THESSALONIANS 1:1-4**	*Gospel came to them in power* **1 THESSALONIANS 1:5-10**	*How true ministers should preach* **1 THESSALONIANS 2:1-5**
How true ministers should preach **1 THESSALONIANS 2:6-12**	*Converts are glory and joy of missionaries* **1 THESSALONIANS 2:13-20**	*Good tidings* **1 THESSALONIANS 3:1-7**
Perfect that which is lacking in your faith **1 THESSALONIANS 3:8-10**	*Love One Another* **1 THESSALONIANS 3:11-13**	*Make yourselves holy* **1 THESSALONIANS 4:1-8**
Love one another **1 THESSALONIANS 4:9-12**	*The Lord will come and the dead will rise* **1 THESSALONIANS 4:13-18**	*The Saints will know the season of the Second Coming* **1 THESSALONIANS 5:1-6**

The Saints will know the season of the Second Coming **1 THESSALONIANS 5:7-11**	*How saints should live* **1 THESSALONIANS 5:12-19**	*How saints should live* **1 THESSALONIANS 5:20-28**
Greeting **2 THESSALONIANS 1:1-6**	*Second Coming is a day of vengeance* **2 THESSALONIANS 1:7-12**	*Apostasy will precede Second Coming* **2 THESSALONIANS 2:1-2**
Satan will be revealed **2 THESSALONIANS 2:3-8**	*Satan will be revealed* **2 THESSALONIANS 2:9-12**	*Gospel prepares for eternal glory* **2 THESSALONIANS 2:13-17**
Pray for triumph of gospel **2 THESSALONIANS 3:1-5**	*Importance of work* **2 THESSALONIANS 3:6-12**	*Be not weary in well doing* **2 THESSALONIANS 3:13-18**

October 21–27

Study these sections in *Come, Follow Me—For Individuals and Families: New Testament 2019.* As you study, record the teachings that stand out to you as well as any impressions you may receive. Be sure to make notes of any doctrines or principles you would like to discuss as a family in family home evening, family scripture study or in another setting.

1 *Ministers of the gospel preach with sincerity and love.*

1 Thessalonians 1–2

2 *As I follow Jesus Christ, I can become holy.*

1 Thessalonians 3:9–4:12

3 *If I am faithful and watchful, I will be prepared for the Savior's Second Coming.*

1 Thessalonians 4:16–18; 5:1–10;
2 Thessalonians 1:4–10

4 *An apostasy, or falling away from truth, was prophesied to precede the Second Coming.*

2 Thessalonians 2

FAMILY HOME EVENING • FAMILY SCRIPTURE STUDY

MAKE A PLAN

In the space below, make a plan on WHAT and HOW you would like to teach your family. As you plan, prayerfully consider each member of the family with their learning levels and personal needs. Also, consider how different family members can contribute to the teaching of the rest of the family. They could make visual aids, study a particular topic and prepare to teach the family, research something, etc.

TEACHING IDEAS FOR YOU:

- To teach about the characteristics and experiences that missionaries might have, you could do the following.

1. Did you or someone in your family serve a mission? Start by telling a favorite experience from your (or their) mission.
2. Explain that Paul gave a list of some qualities of a true minister, or missionary. Have everyone turn to 1 Thessalonians 2:2-12.
3. On a poster board, have your children draw a missionary in the middle of the poster, leaving plenty of space to write and draw things around the missionary. Under the missionary make a list of people your family knows who have served missions or are serving missions. You could also write the name of your local missionaries.
4. Starting in 1 Thessalonians 2:2, have your family identify a quality of a good missionary (in verse 2, Paul said that they were bold in speaking the gospel to the people, even when it was received with contention). Talk about what this means and an experience you may have had doing the same. You could talk about the importance of not being shy, or scared when sharing the gospel, and not apologizing for the truth you know. You could also talk about how to do this in a loving way.
5. Have your children draw a picture on the poster board that represents the quality in verse 2, and then write about what they learned in their personal journals.
6. Continue looking for principles in verses 3-12, and discussing, drawing, and writing about each of them.

* Fun Idea: If you or someone in your family served a mission, for dinner make a meal that you had frequently on your mission.

* With Christmas approaching, you could talk about what you can do for your local missionaries, the missionaries from your ward that are serving, or any missionaries you know personally in your family or friends' families.

* Schedule the missionaries to come for dinner in your home.

* Talk to your children about how they can prepare to be missionaries like the one on the poster. You could also show the video on the Church's website called, "Missionary Song Medley," which shows various children and youth doing things that will prepare them to serve a mission.

1 AND 2 TIMOTHY; TITUS; PHILEMON

Be Thou an Example of the Believers

OCTOBER 28–NOVEMBER 3

As you study each set of verses, use the boxes to record what you are learning. Record the spiritual impressions you receive, the doctrinal truths you find, questions that come to mind, specific things you would like to teach your family, favorite phrases, etc. You can write, draw pictures, make diagrams... There is no right or wrong way.

Greeting **1 TIMOTHY 1:1-2**	*Teach only true doctrine* **1 TIMOTHY 1:3-11**	*Christ came to save sinners* **1 TIMOTHY 1:12-17**	*War a good warfare* **1 TIMOTHY 1:18-20**
We should pray for all men **1 TIMOTHY 2:1-4**	*Christ is our mediator* **1 TIMOTHY 2:5-7**	*Women should dress modestly* **1 TIMOTHY 2:8-10**	*Women blessed in child bearing* **1 TIMOTHY 2:11-15**
Qualifications for bishops **1 TIMOTHY 3:1-7**	*Qualifications for deacons* **1 TIMOTHY 3:8-13**	*The Church of the Living God* **1 TIMOTHY 3:14-16**	*The latter-day apostasy* **1 TIMOTHY 4:1-6**
Christ is the Savior of all men **1 TIMOTHY 4:7-11**	*How to be an example of believers* **1 TIMOTHY 4:12-16**	*Saints to care for worthy poor* **1 TIMOTHY 5:1-18**	*Policies concerning elders* **1 TIMOTHY 5:19-25**
Teach sound doctrine only **1 TIMOTHY 6:1-6**	*The love of money* **1 TIMOTHY 6:7-10**	*Fight the good fight* **1 TIMOTHY 6:11-18**	*Trust not in riches* **1 TIMOTHY 6:19-21**

Greeting **2 TIMOTHY 1:1-6**	*God hath not given us the spirit of fear* **2 TIMOTHY 1:7-9**	*Christ brings immortality and eternal life* **2 TIMOTHY 1:10-11**	*Hold fast* **2 TIMOTHY 1:12-18**
Be strong **2 TIMOTHY 2:1-7**	*Christ gives eternal glory to the elect* **2 TIMOTHY 2:8-13**	*Shun contention, seek godliness* **2 TIMOTHY 2:14-26**	*Apostasy and perilous times in last days* **2 TIMOTHY 3:1-13**
The scriptures guide us in salvation **2 TIMOTHY 3:14-17**	*Latter-day ministers should preach gospel* **2 TIMOTHY 4:1-5**	*Assurance of exaltation* **2 TIMOTHY 4:6-22**	*Greeting* **TITUS 1:1-4**
Bishops must be blameless **TITUS 1:5-9**	*Many vain talkers* **TITUS 1:10-12**	*Rebuke them sharply* **TITUS 1:13-16**	*Deny ungodliness* **TITUS 2:1-15**
Live righteously after baptism **TITUS 3:1-7**	*Live righteously after baptism* **TITUS 3:8-15**	*Greeting* **PHILEMON 1:1-7**	*The gospel changes a servant into a brother* **PHILEMON 1:8-25**

Study these sections in *Come, Follow Me—For Individuals and Families: New Testament 2019.* As you study, record the teachings that stand out to you as well as any impressions you may receive. Be sure to make notes of any doctrines or principles you would like to discuss as a family in family home evening, family scripture study or in another setting.

1 *Who were Timothy and Titus?*

1 and 2 Timothy; Titus

2 *If I am "an example of the believers," I can lead others to the Savior and His gospel.*

1 Timothy 4:10–16

3 *"God hath not given us the spirit of fear; but of power, and of love, and of a sound mind."*

2 Timothy

4 *Living the gospel provides safety from the spiritual dangers of the last days.*

2 Timothy 3

5 *Who was Philemon?*

Philemon

6 *Followers of Christ forgive one another.*

Philemon

FAMILY HOME EVENING • FAMILY SCRIPTURE STUDY

MAKE A PLAN

In the space below, make a plan on WHAT and HOW you would like to teach your family. As you plan, prayerfully consider each member of the family with their learning levels and personal needs. Also, consider how different family members can contribute to the teaching of the rest of the family. They could make visual aids, study a particular topic and prepare to teach the family, research something, etc.

TEACHING IDEAS FOR YOU:

- You can teach your children about being "an example of the believers" (1 Timothy 4:12) with the following ideas.
  1. Set out a dessert that needs to be sliced (like a cake or pie).
  2. Ask who wants a piece and when you serve it to them, take a handful out and sloppily put it on their plate.
  3. Ask who else wants one, and this time give them a nice slice of the dessert.
  4. Serve everyone else, wash your hands, and then ask them to tell you which is the better way to be served (even though they will probably laugh about the sloppy way, they wouldn't want you to do that if their friends were over or if you were serving at a nice event).
  5. Have everyone turn to 1 Timothy 4:12 and read it together. Liken the dessert to this scripture by explaining that just like the cake is a delicious dessert that you wanted to have, it matters how it is served. We took upon the name of Christ when we were baptized and we are walking, talking examples of the gospel of Jesus Christ. If someone is watching us (i.e. the cake) while considering the gospel, and we are a bad example, they may no longer be interested.
  6. In everyone's journals have them make six boxes and in each box write one of the ways Paul said that we need to be an example (word, conversation, charity, spirit, faith, purity). Have everyone write or draw pictures of what we should and should not do to be an example of believers in each of those six ways. They could also talk about a person they know who is a good example in each of those six ways.
     * Tip: The *For the Strength of Youth* pamphlet is an excellent resource for things we should and should not do.
  7. Have everyone memorize this scripture, or do their best to be able to repeat it in their own words.
  8. Encourage everyone to make a goal of at least one way they will be a better example of the believers.

HEBREWS 1-6

Jesus Christ, "the Author of Eternal Salvation"

NOVEMBER 4-10

As you study each set of verses, use the boxes to record what you are learning. Record the spiritual impressions you receive, the doctrinal truths you find, questions that come to mind, specific things you would like to teach your family, favorite phrases, etc. You can write, draw pictures, make diagrams... There is no right or wrong way.

Christ is in the image of His father **HEBREWS 1:1-4**	*Christ is a god, angels are ministering spirits* **HEBREWS 1:5-14**	*Jesus came to suffer death* **HEBREWS 2:1-9**
Christ came to save man **HEBREWS 2:10-18**	*Christ is the Apostle and High Priest* **HEBREWS 3:1**	*Christ is the Son who made the house* **HEBREWS 3:2-6**
Now is the time and day of your salvation **HEBREWS 3:7-12**	*Now is the time and day of your salvation* **HEBREWS 3:13-19**	*The gospel was offered to ancient Israel* **HEBREWS 4:1-2**

Enter into the rest of the Lord **HEBREWS 4:3-11**	*Word of God is powerful* **HEBREWS 4:12-13**	*Jesus was tempted in all points and was still without sin* **HEBREWS 4:14-16**
Priesthood holders must be called of God **HEBREWS 5:1-4**	*Christ was a priest* **HEBREWS 5:5-10**	*Ministers should be able to understand and teach difficult doctrines* **HEBREWS 5:11-14**
Let us go onto perfection **HEBREWS 6:1-3**	*Sons of perdition* **HEBREWS 6:4-9**	*God swears with an oath that the faithful will be saved* **HEBREWS 6:10-20**

November 4–10

Study these sections in *Come, Follow Me—For Individuals and Families: New Testament 2019.* As you study, record the teachings that stand out to you as well as any impressions you may receive. Be sure to make notes of any doctrines or principles you would like to discuss as a family in family home evening, family scripture study or in another setting.

1 *Who wrote the Epistle to the Hebrews?*

Hebrews

2 *Jesus Christ is "the express image" of Heavenly Father.*

Hebrews 1–5

3 *Jesus Christ suffered temptation and infirmities so that He can understand and help me.*

Hebrews 2:9–18; 4:12–16; 5:7–8

4 *In order to receive God's blessings, I must "harden not" my heart.*

Hebrews 3:7–4:11

FAMILY HOME EVENING • FAMILY SCRIPTURE STUDY

MAKE A PLAN

In the space below, make a plan on WHAT and HOW you would like to teach your family. As you plan, prayerfully consider each member of the family with their learning levels and personal needs. Also, consider how different family members can contribute to the teaching of the rest of the family. They could make visual aids, study a particular topic and prepare to teach the family, research something, etc.

TEACHING IDEAS FOR YOU:

- Hebrews is a wonderful book to teach about the Savior, Jesus Christ. Paul wrote the Epistle to the Hebrews to help Jewish members of the Church maintain their faith in Jesus Christ and not to return to their former ways (see Hebrews 10:32–38). To help your children build on their own personal knowledge of Jesus Christ, you could do some or all of the following:

1. Print a beautiful picture of Jesus Christ and paste it in the center of a poster board.
2. Around the picture, have your children write or draw everything they know about Jesus Christ. Encourage them to be as specific as possible.
3. Have them look up some of the scriptures in Hebrews where they might learn something new about Jesus Christ. Have them add to the poster whenever they learn something. Some suggestions are:
    - Hebrews 1:1-4 (Christ is in the image of His father)
    - Hebrews 1:5-14 (Christ is a God, He is above the angels)
    - Hebrews 2:1-9 (Christ came to suffer death)
    - Hebrews 2:10-18 (Christ came to save man)
    - Hebrews 3:1 (Christ is the Apostle and High Priest)
    - Hebrews 4:14-16 (Christ was tempted in all things and was still without sin)
4. Invite everyone to write their testimonies of Jesus Christ in their journals and include in their testimonies some things that they put on the poster. Give everyone time to share all or part of their testimonies.
5. Do you have a favorite song, poem, or piece of art about Jesus Christ? Share this with your family and express why it is touching or special to you. Have others also share their favorite song, poem, or piece of art.

* Fun idea: Invite everyone to create their own piece of art expressing part of their testimony of Jesus Christ.

HEBREWS 7–13

An High Priest of Good Things to Come

NOVEMBER 11-17

As you study each set of verses, use the boxes to record what you are learning. Record the spiritual impressions you receive, the doctrinal truths you find, questions that come to mind, specific things you would like to teach your family, favorite phrases, etc. You can write, draw pictures, make diagrams... There is no right or wrong way.

Who was Melchizedek? **HEBREWS 7:1-3**	*Abraham paid Melchizedek tithes* **HEBREWS 7:4-10**	*Melchizedek Priesthood needed to administer the gospel* **HEBREWS 7:11-14**	*Power of endless lives* **HEBREWS 7:15-17**
Melchizedek Priesthood received with oath and covenant **HEBREWS 7:18-22**	*Salvation comes through intercession of Melchizedek Priesthood* **HEBREWS 7:23-28**	*Christ offered Himself a sacrifice for sin* **HEBREWS 8:1-5**	*God promised to make a new covenant with Israel* **HEBREWS 8:6-13**
Mosaic ordinances pointed to Christ **HEBREWS 9:1-10**	*Christ came and redeemed us* **HEBREWS 9:11-14**	*Christ is the mediator of the new covenant* **HEBREWS 9:15-28**	*We are sanctified by blood of Christ* **HEBREWS 10:1-18**
Those who fall from grace **HEBREWS 10:19-37**	*The just live by faith* **HEBREWS 10:38-39**	*Faith* **HEBREWS 11:1-3**	*Abel's faith* **HEBREWS 11:4**

Enoch's faith **HEBREWS 11:5-6**	*Noah's faith* **HEBREWS 11:7**	*Abraham & Sara's faith* **HEBREWS 11:8-19**	*Isaac's faith* **HEBREWS 11:20**
Jacob's faith **HEBREWS 11:21**	*Joseph's faith* **HEBREWS 11:22**	*Moses' faith* **HEBREWS 11:23-29**	*The faith of others* **HEBREWS 11:30-40**
The loved are chastened **HEBREWS 12:1-8**	*God is the Father of our spirits* **HEBREWS 12:9-10**	*Follow peace and holiness* **HEBREWS 12:11-17**	*Exalted saints belong to Church of the Firstborn* **HEBREWS 12:18-24**
A kingdom which cannot be moved **HEBREWS 12:25-29**	*Marriage is honorable in all* **HEBREWS 13:1-7**	*How Christians offer sacrifices* **HEBREWS 13:8-17**	*Farewell* **HEBREWS 13:18-25**

Study these sections in *Come, Follow Me—For Individuals and Families: New Testament 2019.* As you study, record the teachings that stand out to you as well as any impressions you may receive. Be sure to make notes of any doctrines or principles you would like to discuss as a family in family home evening, family scripture study or in another setting.

1 *The Melchizedek Priesthood is the higher priesthood.*

Hebrews 7:1–22

2 *Ancient and modern ordinances point to Jesus Christ.*

Hebrews 9:1–10:22

3 *Faith requires trusting in God's promises.*

Hebrews 11

FAMILY HOME EVENING • FAMILY SCRIPTURE STUDY

MAKE A PLAN

In the space below, make a plan on WHAT and HOW you would like to teach your family. As you plan, prayerfully consider each member of the family with their learning levels and personal needs. Also, consider how different family members can contribute to the teaching of the rest of the family. They could make visual aids, study a particular topic and prepare to teach the family, research something, etc.

TEACHING IDEAS FOR YOU:

- Here are some ideas to teach about "faith," and Hebrews 11.

1. Put a stack of feathers, a lit lamp (plugged in), and a remote-controlled item (like a car or flying helicopter) on the table, and ask everyone what these three things have in common.
2. Give each person a feather and tell them that you would like to see who can keep the feather in the air (by blowing it, no hands allowed) the longest. After a couple of minutes, ask them how they kept the feather in the air (by blowing it). Tell them that you could not see the air they were blowing, so how can you know that they have air in their mouth? (The *evidence* of the feather staying in the air!). Ask them why you should believe something you cannot see (because we can see the evidences).
3. Point to the lamp on the table. Ask your family, "How does that lamp light up?" (electricity). Explain that you cannot see the electricity, so how can you know electricity is real? (the evidence of the light coming from the lamp).
4. Make the remote-controlled item go. Ask how that item is able to move (the power from the batteries). Explain that you cannot see the power from the batteries so maybe the power isn't real. They should now respond that you can know it is real because you can see the evidence of the item moving.
5. Open up to Hebrews 11:1. Read and talk about what that scripture is teaching, and have everyone write the scripture in their personal journals and also write about what the scripture means.
6. Talk about how faith is a real and true power and can cause things to happen. You may not be able to see faith, but you will see evidences of faith.
7. Explain that in chapter 11 Paul talks about several people from the scriptures who did amazing things because of their faith. Have everyone look through their scriptures and circle everyone's names they can find.
8. Tell everyone to pick someone and draw a picture of them (but do not let anyone see what they are drawing) and then have everyone display their pictures while everyone guesses who they drew.
9. Tell a story about when faith was a power in your life, and bear your testimony of the importance of having faith. Let everyone else share a story of when they had faith.

* You might want to make a list of things each family member can do to help their faith grow.

JAMES

Be Ye Doers of the Word, and Not Hearers Only

NOVEMBER 18–24

As you study each set of verses, use the boxes to record what you are learning. Record the spiritual impressions you receive, the doctrinal truths you find, questions that come to mind, specific things you would like to teach your family, favorite phrases, etc. You can write, draw pictures, make diagrams... There is no right or wrong way.

Ask of God for wisdom **JAMES 1:1-7**	*A double minded man* **JAMES 1:8-12**	*Resist temptation* **JAMES 1:13-16**
Every good gift **JAMES 1:17-18**	*The wrath of man* **JAMES 1:19-20**	*Be doers* **JAMES 1:22-25**
Pure religion **JAMES 1:26-27**	*Respect the poor* **JAMES 2:1-9**	*Live the whole law* **JAMES 2:10-13**
Faith without works is dead **JAMES 2:14-18**	*Faith without works is dead* **JAMES 2:19-21**	*Faith without works is dead* **JAMES 2:22-24**

Faith without works is dead **JAMES 2:25-26**	*Tame thy tongue* **JAMES 3:1-5**	*Tame thy tongue* **JAMES 3:6-8**
Tame thy tongue **JAMES 3:9-13**	*Envy and strife* **JAMES 3:14-18**	*Why wars happen* **JAMES 4:1-3**
Enemies of God **JAMES 4:4-6**	*Submit yourselves to God* **JAMES 4:7-12**	*What sin is* **JAMES 4:13-17**
Misery awaits the rich **JAMES 5:1-6**	*Be patient as you wait for Christ's coming* **JAMES 5:7-11**	*Elders heal the sick* **JAMES 5:12-20**

November 18-24

Study these sections in *Come, Follow Me—For Individuals and Families: New Testament 2019.* As you study, record the teachings that stand out to you as well as any impressions you may receive. Be sure to make notes of any doctrines or principles you would like to discuss as a family in family home evening, family scripture study or in another setting.

1 *Who was James?*

James

2 *Patient endurance leads to perfection.*

James 1:2–4; 5:7–11

3 *Faith requires action.*

James 1:3–8, 21–25; 2:14–26; 4:17

4 *The words I speak have the power to hurt or bless others.*

James 1:26; 3:1–18

5 *As a disciple of Jesus Christ, I should love all people, regardless of their circumstances.*

James 2:1–9

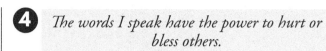

FAMILY HOME EVENING • FAMILY SCRIPTURE STUDY

MAKE A PLAN

In the space below, make a plan on WHAT and HOW you would like to teach your family. As you plan, prayerfully consider each member of the family with their learning levels and personal needs. Also, consider how different family members can contribute to the teaching of the rest of the family. They could make visual aids, study a particular topic and prepare to teach the family, research something, etc.

TEACHING IDEAS FOR YOU:

- To teach James 1:5-6, consider doing the following:

1. Begin by watching the video titled "The Restoration" found on the Church's website (search "The Restoration video." It is 19 minutes and 12 seconds.
2. After the video ask everyone to share the part of the video that touched them the most.
3. Invite everyone to turn to James 1:5-6 and read it together. Discuss the scripture and look up any words that others may not understand.
4. Discuss how much of a difference this scripture made in Joseph Smith's life, and the lives of countless others on both sides of the veil.
5. Have everyone make three columns in their personal journals. Have them label the first column "past," the second column "present," and the third column "future."
6. Invite everyone to think of a time in their past when they asked of God for an answer and they were given direction. Tell them to write (or draw) about it in the first column and then share their experience with everyone.
7. In the second column write "present," and ask them to write or draw about something that they are currently praying about. Invite them to share.
8. In the third column write "past," and invite them to make a list of things in their future they will need to answers for. Discuss everyone's lists.
9. Bear your testimony about the power of prayer.
10. Encourage everyone to memorize James 1:5-6.

1 AND 2 PETER

Rejoice with Joy Unspeakable and Full of Glory

NOVEMBER 25 - DECEMBER 1

As you study each set of verses, use the boxes to record what you are learning. Record the spiritual impressions you receive, the doctrinal truths you find, questions that come to mind, specific things you would like to teach your family, favorite phrases, etc. You can write, draw pictures, make diagrams... There is no right or wrong way.

Greeting **1 PETER 1:1-2**	*Trials of faith are precious* **1 PETER 1:3-9**	*All prophets prophesied of Christ* **1 PETER 1:10-12**	*Be ye holy* **1 PETER 1:13-16**
Christ foreordained to be Redeemer **1 PETER 1:17-21**	*Ye have purified your souls* **1 PETER 1:22-25**	*Converts are newborn babes in Christ* **1 PETER 2:1-3**	*Christ is the Chief Cornerstone* **1 PETER 2:4-8**
A royal priesthood **1 PETER 2:9-10**	*Abstain from lusts* **1 PETER 2:11-12**	*We are subject to man's laws* **1 PETER 2:13-19**	*We are subject to man's laws* **1 PETER 2:20-25**
Husbands and wives should love each other **1 PETER 3:1-7**	*Live by gospel standards* **1 PETER 3:8-17**	*Christ preached to the spirits in prison* **1 PETER 3:18-22**	*Gain the mind of Christ* **1 PETER 4:1-2**

The world thinks we are strange for not doing as they do **1 PETER 4:3-5**	*Why the gospel is preached to the dead* **1 PETER 4:6**	*Speak as oracles of God* **1 PETER 4:7-11**	*The righteous will be tested in all things* **1 PETER 4:12-19**
Elders are to feed God's flock **1 PETER 5:1-4**	*Humble yourselves* **1 PETER 5:5-11**	*Farewell* **1 PETER 5:12-14**	*Be partakers of the divine nature* **2 PETER 1:1-9**
Saints should make their calling and election sure **2 PETER 1:10-18**	*Prophecy comes by power of the Holy Ghost* **2 PETER 1:19-21**	*False teachers* **2 PETER 2:1-8**	*God knows how to deliver us from temptation* **2 PETER 2:9**
Lustful saints perish in their own corruption **2 PETER 2:10-15**	*Lustful saints perish in their own corruption* **2 PETER 2:16-22**	*Latter-day scoffers deny Second Coming* **2 PETER 3:1-9**	*Elements to melt at Second Coming* **2 PETER 3:10-18**

November 25 - December 1

Study these sections in *Come, Follow Me—For Individuals and Families: New Testament 2019*. As you study, record the teachings that stand out to you as well as any impressions you may receive. Be sure to make notes of any doctrines or principles you would like to discuss as a family in family home evening, family scripture study or in another setting.

1 *I can find joy during times of trial and suffering.*

1 Peter 1:3–9; 2:19–24; 3:14–17; 4:12–19

2 *The gospel is preached to the dead so they can be judged justly.*

1 Peter 3:18–20; 4:1–6

3 *Through the power of Jesus Christ, I can develop my divine nature.*

2 Peter 1:1–11

FAMILY HOME EVENING • FAMILY SCRIPTURE STUDY

MAKE A PLAN

In the space below, make a plan on WHAT and HOW you would like to teach your family. As you plan, prayerfully consider each member of the family with their learning levels and personal needs. Also, consider how different family members can contribute to the teaching of the rest of the family. They could make visual aids, study a particular topic and prepare to teach the family, research something, etc.

TEACHING IDEAS FOR YOU:

- To teach 1 Peter 3:18-20 and 1 Peter 4:6 (Jesus taught the spirits in spirit prison, you could do the following:

1. Have the children draw the plan of salvation on a poster or in their journals.
2. Ask them to label each part of the plan, and write or draw everything that they know about each part of the plan (for example, they could write or draw about the War in Heaven or Council in Heaven in the Premortal Life.
3. After they have finished, tell them that today they are going to learn more about the Spirit World. Next to the Spirit World, have them list people they know who are there right now.
4. Open the scriptures to 1 Peter 3:18-20 and 4:6. Read about Christ in the Spirit World. You can also read D&C 138. Have your children write or draw what they learned on their Plan of Savlation drawing.
5. Explain that missionary work has continued in the Spirit World ever since then. Share the following quote:

> *"When the Gospel is preached to the spirits in prison, the success attending that preaching will be far greater than that attending the preaching of our Elders in this life. I believe there will be very few indeed of those spirits who will not gladly receive the Gospel when it is carried to them. The circumstances there will be a thousand times more favorable"* (President Lorenzo Snow, "Discourse by President Lorenzo Snow," *Millennial Star,* Jan. 22, 1894, 50).

6. Talk about why this doctrine is comforting to us while we are here on earth. Also discuss those you know who are in the Spirit World at this moment.
7. Help your children understand that although a spirit might accept the gospel in the Spirit World, they need our help to receive the ordinances they want and need. Share the following with them (and have them add the information to their drawings):

> **The Spirit World: Paradise and Spirit Prison**
> *The spirit world is divided into paradise and spirit prison. The people who were baptized and stayed faithful in their mortal life go to paradise. This is a place of rest, peace, and joy. Jesus Christ visited and taught the spirits in paradise between His death and Resurrection (see D&C 138:18–27).*
> *Good people who died without gospel knowledge go to spirit prison. This is also where those who were disobedient or wicked in their mortal lives go. Righteous spirits teach the gospel to these people, and they then have the chance to accept the gospel and repent (see D&C 138:28–37). Without a body, though, they can't get baptized or participate in the other ordinances necessary to receive eternal life. (See Alma 40:14.)*
> **Proxy Ordinances**
> *Fortunately, Heavenly Father is merciful, loving, and just, so He provides a way for all His children to be saved. This is where you can help. When you perform proxy ordinances for people, they have the chance to accept these ordinances. You can do for them what they can't do for themselves on their path to eternal life. These repentant souls can "be redeemed, through obedience to the ordinances of the house of God" (D&C 138:58; see also verse 59). And you can experience the great joy that comes from helping someone in spirit prison receive these essential ordinances.*
> ** March 2016 Ensign*

8. Look for ancestors in your family who might have accepted the gospel in the Spirit World and might be waiting for someone in their family to do their work. Come up with a plan on how everyone can learn how to do Family History and participate in this important work.

1-3 JOHN; JUDE

God is love

DECEMBER 2-8

As you study each set of verses, use the boxes to record what you are learning. Record the spiritual impressions you receive, the doctrinal truths you find, questions that come to mind, specific things you would like to teach your family, favorite phrases, etc. You can write, draw pictures, make diagrams... There is no right or wrong way.

Obedience brings fellowship with God **1 JOHN 1:1-7**	*Confess our sins* **1 JOHN 1:8-10**	*Christ is our Advocate* **1 JOHN 2:1-2**	*We know God by obedience* **1 JOHN 2:3-6**
Love your brother **1 JOHN 2:7-14**	*Love not the world* **1 JOHN 2:15-17**	*Antichrists in last days* **1 JOHN 2:18-26**	*Abide in Him* **1 JOHN 2:27-29**
Sons of God shall be like Christ **1 JOHN 3:1-3**	*How to tell righteous from wicked* **1 JOHN 3:4-10**	*Love one another* **1 JOHN 3:11-18**	*Obedience brings answers to prayers* **1 JOHN 3:19-24**
Try the spirits **1 JOHN 4:1-6**	*God is love* **1 JOHN 4:7-10**	*God is love* **1 JOHN 4:11-14**	*God is love* **1 JOHN 4:15-18**

God is love **1 JOHN 4:19-21**	*Saints born of God* **1 JOHN 5:1-5**	*Water, blood, and Spirit* **1 JOHN 5:6-9**	*Believe in Christ to receive eternal life* **1 JOHN 5:10-21**
Greeting **2 JOHN 1:1-3**	*Bring up children in light & truth* **2 JOHN 1:4**	*This is love* **2 JOHN 1:5-6**	*Look to yourselves* **2 JOHN 1:7-9**
Turn away those who do not bring true doctrine **2 JOHN 1:10-13**	*Help those who love truth* **3 JOHN 1:1-7**	*Help those who love truth* **3 JOHN 1:8-14**	*Contend for the faith* **JUDE 1:1-5**
Some angels did not keep first estate **JUDE 1:6**	*Michael disputed with devil* **JUDE 1:7-13**	*Enoch prophesied of Second Coming* **JUDE 1:14-16**	*Mockers will come in last days* **JUDE 1:17-25**

1-3 John; Jude

December 2-8

Study these sections in *Come, Follow Me—For Individuals and Families: New Testament 2019.* As you study, record the teachings that stand out to you as well as any impressions you may receive. Be sure to make notes of any doctrines or principles you would like to discuss as a family in family home evening, family scripture study or in another setting.

1 *God is light, and God is love.*

1 John

2 *I can become like Jesus Christ.*

1 John 2:24–3:3

3 *Has "no man … seen God at any time"?*

Joseph Smith Translation, 1 John 4:12

4 *As I exercise faith in Jesus Christ and am born again, I can overcome the world.*

1 John 5

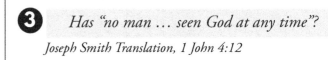

FAMILY HOME EVENING • FAMILY SCRIPTURE STUDY

MAKE A PLAN

In the space below, make a plan on WHAT and HOW you would like to teach your family. As you plan, prayerfully consider each member of the family with their learning levels and personal needs. Also, consider how different family members can contribute to the teaching of the rest of the family. They could make visual aids, study a particular topic and prepare to teach the family, research something, etc.

TEACHING IDEAS FOR YOU:

- Did the Church announce a Christmas campaign this year like in years past? If it is centered on serving others, there are some great scriptures in this week's chapters that would apply beautifully. Teach your children about the Christmas campaign and tell them that you are going to make some Christmas scripture art to hang in the home to help remind us why we should serve others. Write the scripture references (some suggestions below) on the top of pieces of paper (one reference per paper) and have your children study them and write or draw what they teach on each poster. Tell them to include some festive Christmas designs as they create the art.

Some scriptures you could use are:

- 1 John 2:10-11 (Love your brother)
- 1 John 2:15-17 (Love not the world)
- 1 John 3:11-17 (Love one another)
- 1 John 4:7-21 (God is love)

After you have made the posters, make a specific plan concerning whom you will serve this Christmas and what you are going to do. Invite everyone to write their favorite scripture from the lesson in their personal journals, as well as their individual or family's plan for service this Christmas.

REVELATION 1-11

Glory, and Power, Be unto … the Lamb for Ever

DECEMBER 9–15

As you study each set of verses, use the boxes to record what you are learning. Record the spiritual impressions you receive, the doctrinal truths you find, questions that come to mind, specific things you would like to teach your family, favorite phrases, etc. You can write, draw pictures, make diagrams... There is no right or wrong way.

Christ chooses kings and priests **REVELATION 1:1-6**	*Christ shall come again* **REVELATION 1:7-8**	*Ancient saints* **REVELATION 1:9-11**	*John sees the risen Lord* **REVELATION 1:12-20**
Overcome and inherit Celestial Kingdom **REVELATION 2:1-17**	*Overcome and rule many kingdoms* **REVELATION 2:18-29**	*Overcome and retain name in Book of Life* **REVELATION 3:1-6**	*Overcome and reach godhood* **REVELATION 3:7-13**
Overcome and be wtih Jesus on throne **REVELATION 3:14-22**	*John sees Celestial earth and throne of God* **REVELATION 4:1-11**	*Book with seven seals* **REVELATION 5:1-4**	*Christ takes book* **REVELATION 5:5-7**
Every creature praises God & lamb **REVELATION 5:8-14**	*First seal opened* **REVELATION 6:1-2**	*Second seal opened* **REVELATION 6:3-4**	*Third seal opened* **REVELATION 6:5-6**

Fourth seal opened **REVELATION 6:7-8**	*Fifth seal opened* **REVELATION 6:9-11**	*Sixth seal opened / signs of the times* **REVELATION 6:12-17**	*Gospel restored* **REVELATION 7:1**
The sealing of 144,000 **REVELATION 7:2-8**	*The hosts of the exalted from all nations* **REVELATION 7:9-17**	*Seventh seal opened* **REVELATION 8:1**	*Fire & desolation poured out preceding the Second Coming* **REVELATION 8:2-13**
Wars and plagues **REVELATION 9:1-7**	*Wars and plagues* **REVELATION 9:8-14**	*Wars and plagues* **REVELATION 9:15-21**	*John participates in restoration of all things* **REVELATION 10:1-11**
Two prophets slain in Jerusalem **REVELATION 11:1-5**	*Two prophets slain in Jerusalem* **REVELATION 11:6-10**	*Two prophets slain in Jerusalem* **REVELATION 11:11-14**	*Christ shall reign over all earth* **REVELATION 11:15-19**

December 9–15

Study these sections in *Come, Follow Me—For Individuals and Families: New Testament 2019*. As you study, record the teachings that stand out to you as well as any impressions you may receive. Be sure to make notes of any doctrines or principles you would like to discuss as a family in family home evening, family scripture study or in another setting.

1 *How can I make sense of the book of Revelation?*

Revelation

2 *John's vision teaches how Heavenly Father saves His children.*

Revelation

3 *Jesus Christ knows me personally and will help me overcome my challenges.*

Revelation 2–3

4 *Only Jesus Christ could make Heavenly Father's plan possible.*

Revelation 5

5 *The Restoration preceded the destruction that will take place before the Second Coming of Jesus Christ.*

Revelation 6–11

FAMILY HOME EVENING • FAMILY SCRIPTURE STUDY

MAKE A PLAN

In the space below, make a plan on WHAT and HOW you would like to teach your family. As you plan, prayerfully consider each member of the family with their learning levels and personal needs. Also, consider how different family members can contribute to the teaching of the rest of the family. They could make visual aids, study a particular topic and prepare to teach the family, research something, etc.

TEACHING IDEAS FOR YOU:

- To teach about the seven seals, take seven pieces of paper and roll them and put a sticker (seal) on the seam to hold the roll shut. Label the first scroll one, the second scroll two, and so on until scroll number seven. In his vision, John saw figurative representations of some of the major events pertaining to each of the 1,000-year time periods represented by the seven seals. Starting in Revelation 6:1-2, have the children open up seal #1 and draw a simple picture of what was written on that seal. Continue until you get to seal number six. You can find some explanations of what the different seals represent on the Church's website.

Explain that the sixth seal represents our own time and the events, particularly the calamities, leading up to the Millennium, when Jesus Christ will reign personally on the earth. Have the children write or draw what they find from Revelation 6:12 until Revelation 7:17. Then they can draw what they find on the seventh seal in Revelation 8 through Revelation 11.

Although the events may seem frightening, help your children understand that the Lord gave us this book so that we could be prepared and understand that the world is being prepared for His Second Coming.

Invite everyone to make two columns in their personal journals. In the first column have them write or draw some of the signs and events that are in the sixth and seven seals. In the second column have them write what they can do to be prepared and feel peace while the world is in chaos around them.

As a family discuss what more you can do to make certain your home is a refuge for your family and all that come into your home.

CHRISTMAS

Good Tidings of Great Joy

DECEMBER 16–22

Using your own thoughts and the teachings in *Come, Follow Me—For Individuals and Families: New Testament 2019* ponder and answer the questions below.

1. *Why does the birth of a baby bring so much joy?*

2. *What message did the angel give the shepherds about the Christ child?*

3. *How can you follow Mary's example this Christmas?*

4. *From your studies in the New Testament this year, how did Christ fulfill His mission of redemption?*

5. *How has Christ's mission changed your life?*

Study these sections in *Come, Follow Me—For Individuals and Families: New Testament 2019*. As you study, record the teachings that stand out to you as well as any impressions you may receive. Be sure to make notes of any doctrines or principles you would like to discuss as a family in family home evening, family scripture study or in another setting.

1 JESUS CHRIST CONDESCENDED TO BE BORN AMONG US ON EARTH.

Matthew 1:18–25; 2:1–12; Luke 1:26–38; 2:1–20

❷ JESUS CHRIST FULFILLED HIS MISSION AND MADE IT POSSIBLE FOR ME TO INHERIT ETERNAL LIFE.

1 Corinthians 15:21–26; Colossians 1:12–22; 1 Peter 2:21–25

FAMILY HOME EVENING • FAMILY SCRIPTURE STUDY

MAKE A PLAN

In the space below, make a plan on WHAT and HOW you would like to teach your family. As you plan, prayerfully consider each member of the family with their learning levels and personal needs. Also, consider how different family members can contribute to the teaching of the rest of the family. They could make visual aids, study a particular topic and prepare to teach the family, research something, etc.

TEACHING IDEAS FOR YOU:

- Have a family home evening centered on Christmas hymns. Ask each person to study and come prepared to teach about the history and background of one of the hymns. Invite each person to teach about their hymn and then ask everyone to look through the words in the hymn and share their favorite line and why they chose it. Sing the hymn together or listen to a beautiful arrangement of it. Once you are finished, invite everyone to pick their very favorite line out of all of the hymns you discussed and create a poster with that line, and then display all the posters somewhere in your home.

- Together, watch this year's First Presidency Christmas devotional. You may want to make this memorable and establish some simple traditions while watching this together each year. For example, you could make a hot chocolate bar and set out cozy blankets to use while watching it together. Or you could hand out matching Christmas socks from the dollar store. It could be something simple, but help it stand out.

REVELATION 12–22

He That Overcometh Shall Inherit All Things

DECEMBER 23–29

As you study each set of verses, use the boxes to record what you are learning. Record the spiritual impressions you receive, the doctrinal truths you find, questions that come to mind, specific things you would like to teach your family, favorite phrases, etc. You can write, draw pictures, make diagrams... There is no right or wrong way.

The war on earth between saints and the devil **REVELATION 12:1-6**	*The war on earth began as a war in heaven* **REVELATION 12:7-11**	*The war in heaven continues on earth* **REVELATION 12:12-17**	*Earthly kingdoms controlled by Satan* **REVELATION 13:1-10**
The devil works miracles and deceives men **REVELATION 13:11-18**	*The Lamb shall stand on Mt. Zion* **REVELATION 14:1-5**	*Gospel restored by angels* **REVELATION 14:6-7**	*Punishment awaits wicked* **REVELATION 14:8-11**
Son of man harvests earth **REVELATION 14:12-20**	*Exalted saints praise God in Celestial glory* **REVELATION 15:1-4**	*Plagues upon the wicked* **REVELATION 15:5-8**	*Plagues upon the wicked* **REVELATION 16:1-12**
Nations assemble for Armageddon **REVELATION 16:13-16**	*Christ comes* **REVELATION 16:17-21**	*Babylon the great throughout earth* **REVELATION 17:1-9**	*Babylon the great throughout earth* **REVELATION 17:10-18**

Saints are called out of Babylon **REVELATION 18:1-4**	*Babylon falls* **REVELATION 18:5-24**	*The marriage supper of the lamb* **REVELATION 19:1-9**	*What is the spirit of prophecy?* **REVELATION 19:10**
Christ is King of kings **REVELATION 19:11-16**	*Gather to the supper* **REVELATION 19:17-21**	*Satan bound during Millennium* **REVELATION 20:1-3**	*Saints live & reign with Christ* **REVELATION 20:4-6**
Satan & servants cast out **REVELATION 20:7-10**	*The dead judged out of the books* **REVELATION 20:11-15**	*He that overcomes inherits all things* **REVELATION 21:1-7**	*Earth attains Celestial glory* **REVELATION 21:8-16**
Earth attains Celestial glory **REVELATION 21:17-27**	*Saints reign in Celestial splendor* **REVELATION 22:1-5**	*Christ shall come / men judged* **REVELATION 22:6-16**	*Blessed are they who keep commandments* **REVELATION 22:17-21**

Study these sections in *Come, Follow Me—For Individuals and Families: New Testament 2019*. As you study, record the teachings that stand out to you as well as any impressions you may receive. Be sure to make notes of any doctrines or principles you would like to discuss as a family in family home evening, family scripture study or in another setting.

1 *The War in Heaven continues on earth.*

Revelation 12:7–17

2 *Who is the angel that John saw preaching the gospel?*

Revelation 14:6–7

3 *The Lord invites me to flee Babylon and her sins.*

Revelation 17–18

4 *All of God's children will be judged out of the book of life.*

Revelation 20:12–15

5 *If I am faithful, I will receive celestial glory.*

Revelation 21; 22:1–5

6 *Do these verses mean that there cannot be any additional scripture besides the Bible?*

Revelation 22:18–19

FAMILY HOME EVENING • FAMILY SCRIPTURE STUDY

MAKE A PLAN

In the space below, make a plan on WHAT and HOW you would like to teach your family. As you plan, prayerfully consider each member of the family with their learning levels and personal needs. Also, consider how different family members can contribute to the teaching of the rest of the family. They could make visual aids, study a particular topic and prepare to teach the family, research something, etc.

TEACHING IDEAS FOR YOU:

- To teach your family Revelation 12 and about the War in Heaven, consider the following:

1. Give each person a paper and invite each person to take five minutes and do a simple drawing of Revelation 12:1-4.
2. Ask them what they think this image represents.
3. Explain that the woman represents the Church of God, and the dragon represents Satan and the danger and attacks the Church would face. Read verses 5-6 and explain that the woman fleeing into the wilderness represents the Church entering the Great Apostasy and the priesthood being taken from the earth after the deaths of Jesus Christ and His Apostles.
4. Explain that after the Apostle John saw the dragon threatening the woman and her child, he was shown an event from our premortal life—when Satan and his followers fought against the plan of salvation and the Saints of God. The picture of the vision everyone just drew was merely a continuation on the war in heaven now on earth.
5. Invite your children to study about the war in heaven. Set out paper, markers, and other art supplies. Tell them that you want them to create a display on the table teaching you as much as possible about the war in heaven. They can draw pictures, make diagrams, or create whatever they need to visually teach about that important event. A great resource is to look up "war in heaven" under "Gospel Topics" on the Church's website. Not only is there a description of the war in heaven, but as you scroll down the page there are links to talks and other resources (it will link to the *Encyclopedia of Mormonism* which has a lot of information about the war in heaven).
6. After your family has created a display and taught you all about it, ask them what our greatest weapons were in the war in heaven (we didn't have bodies, so the weapons we use on earth wouldn't have been useful). Look up Revelation 12:11 and determine what our weapons were (*our testimonies*).
7. Point out in Revelation 12:17 that the war in heaven continues here on earth, and Satan makes war with those who keep the commandments of God and have a testimony of Jesus Christ.
8. As a family, make a list of everything you are doing to fight against Satan and make some new goals for the New Year. You may want to especially focus on building your testimonies (your greatest weapon) and making them even stronger.

32943595R00117

Made in the USA
Middletown, DE
09 January 2019